Communications in Computer and Information Science 497

Commenced Publication in 2007
Founding and Former Series Editors:
Alfredo Cuzzocrea, Dominik Ślęzak, and Xiaokang Yang

More information about this series at http://www.springer.com/series/7899

Dimitrios Kotzinos · Yeow Wei Choong
Nicolas Spyratos · Yuzuru Tanaka (Eds.)

Information Search, Integration and Personalization

9th International Workshop, ISIP 2014
Kuala Lumpur, Malaysia, October 9–10, 2014
Revised Selected Papers

 Springer

Editors
Dimitrios Kotzinos
Lab. ETIS, Sciences Informatiques
Université de Cergy-Pontoise
Pontoise
France

Nicolas Spyratos
LRI
University of Paris South
Orsay
France

Yeow Wei Choong
HELP University
Kuala Lumpur
Malaysia

Yuzuru Tanaka
Information Science, Knowledge Media Lab
Hokkaido University
Sapporo, Hokkaido
Japan

ISSN 1865-0929   ISSN 1865-0937 (electronic)
Communications in Computer and Information Science
ISBN 978-3-319-38900-4   ISBN 978-3-319-38901-1 (eBook)
DOI 10.1007/978-3-319-38901-1

Library of Congress Control Number: 2016938668

Printed on acid-free paper

This Springer imprint is published by Springer Nature
The registered company is Springer International Publishing AG Switzerland

Preface

This book contains the selected research papers presented at ISIP 2014, the ninth International Workshop on Information Search, Integration and Personalization. The workshop was held at HELP University, Kuala Lumpur, Malaysia, during October 9–10, 2014.

In addition to a keynote speech given by Professor Kimihito Ito (Hokkaido University, Sapporo, Japan), there were 19 presentations of scientific papers, of which 10 were submitted to the post-workshop peer-review process. The international Program Committee selected six papers to be included in the proceedings. This year we also had an invited paper, allowing us to extend the reach of the workshop to subjects not presented in the workshop but that are on the edge of the research area.

The themes of the presented papers reflected today's diversity of research topics as well as the rapid development of interdisciplinary research. With increasingly sophisticated research in science and technology, there is a growing need for interdisciplinary and international availability, distribution, and exchange of the latest research results, in organic forms, including not only research papers and multimedia documents, but also various tools developed for measurement, analysis, inference, design, planning, simulation, and production as well as the related large data sets. Similar needs are also growing for the interdisciplinary and international availability, distribution, and exchange of ideas and works among artists, musicians, designers, architects, directors, and producers. These contents, including multimedia documents, application tools, and services, are being accumulated on the Web, as well as in local and global databases, at a remarkable speed that we have never experienced with other kinds of publishing media. Large amounts of content are now already on the Web, waiting for their advanced personal and/or public reuse. We need new theories and technologies for the advanced information search, integration through interoperation, and personalization of Web content as well as database content.

The ISIP 2014 workshop was organized to offer a forum for presenting original work and stimulating discussions and exchanges of ideas around these themes, focusing on the following topics:

- Information search in large data sets (databases, digital libraries, data warehouses)
- Comparison of different information search technologies, approaches, and algorithms
- Novel approaches to information search
- Personalized information retrieval and personalized Web search
- Data analytics (data mining, data warehousing)
- Integration of Web-services, knowledge bases, digital libraries
- Federation of smart objects

ISIP started as a series of Franco-Japanese workshops in 2003, and its first edition was placed under the auspices of the French embassy in Tokyo, which provided the financial support along with the JSPS (Japanese Society for the Promotion of Science). Up until 2012, the workshops alternated between Japan and France, and attracted increasing interest from both countries. The following shows the history of past ISIP workshops:

- 2003: First ISIP in Sapporo (June 30–July 2, Meme Media Lab, Hokkaido University, Japan)
- 2005: Second ISIP in Lyon (May 9–11, University Claude Bernard Lyon 1, France)
- 2007: Third ISIP in Sapporo (June 27–30, Meme Media Laboratory, Hokkaido University, Japan)
- 2008: 4th ISIP in Paris (October 6–8, Tour Montparnasse, Paris, France)
- 2009: 5th ISIP in Sapporo (July 6–8, Meme Media Laboratory, Hokkaido University, Japan)
- 2010: 6th ISIP in Lyon (October 11–13, University Claude Bernard Lyon 1, France)
- 2012: 7th ISIP in Sapporo (October 11–13, Meme Media Lab, Hokkaido University, Japan)
- 2013: 8th ISIP in Bangkok (September 16–18, Centara Grand & Bangkok Convention Centre CentralWorld Bangkok, Thailand).

Originally, the workshops were intended for a Franco-Japanese audience, with the occasional invitation of researchers from other countries as keynote speakers. The proceedings of each workshop were published informally, as a technical report of the hosting institution. One exception was the 2005 workshop, selected papers of which were published by the *Journal of Intelligent Information Systems* in its special issue for ISIP 2005 (Vol. 31, Number 2, October 2008). The original goal of the ISIP workshop series was to create close synergies between a selected group of researchers from the two countries; and indeed, several collaborations, joint publications, and joint student supervisions and research projects originated from participants of the workshop.

After the first six workshops, the organizers concluded that the workshop series had reached a mature state with an increasing number of researchers participating every year. As a result, the organizers decided to open up the workshop to a larger audience by inviting speakers from over ten countries at ISIP 2012, ISIP 2013, and ISIP 2014. The effort to attract an even larger international audience will continue in the years to come. This year and last year in particular, an extensive effort was made to include in the Program Committee academics coming from around the globe, giving the workshop an even more international character and disseminating its information and results globally. We expect this to have an important effect in the participation of the workshop in the years to come.

The selected papers contained in this book are grouped into three major topics, namely, information management (where the invited paper is also incuded), information discovery, and knowledge management applications on the web and the cloud; they span major topics in information management research, both modern and traditional.

We would like to express our appreciation to all the staff members of the organizing institution for the help, kindness, and support before during and after the work-shop. And of course we would like to cordially thank all speakers and participants of ISIP 2014 for their intensive discussions and exchange of new ideas. This book is an outcome of those discussions and exchanged ideas.

January 2015

Yeow Wei Choong
Nicolas Spyratos
Yuzuru Tanaka

Organization

ISIP 2014 was organized by the HELP University, Kuala Lumpur, Malaysia.

Executive Committee

Co-chairs

Yeow Wei Choong   HELP University, Malaysia
Nicolas Spyratos   Paris-Sud University, France
Yuzuru Tanaka   Hokkaido University, Japan

Program Committee Chair

Dimitris Kotzinos   University of Cergy-Pontoise, France

Local Organization

Yeow Wei Choong   HELP University, Malaysia

Publicity

Yeow Wei Choong   HELP University, Malaysia
Gilbert Ooi Sin Cheak   HELP University, Malaysia

Program Committee

Adriani, Mina	University of Indonesia, Indonesia
Amann, Bernd	LIP6/UPMC, France
Ba, Hung-Ngo	Can Tho University, Vietnam
Boursier, Patrice	L3i/University of La Rochelle, France
Choong, Yeow-Wei	HELP University, Malaysia
Christophides, Vassilis	University of Crete, Greece
Darmont, Jerome	ERIC/University Lumière Lyon 2, France
d'Orazio, Laurent	LIMOS/Clermont University - University Blaise Pascal, France
Guillet, Fabrice	LINA/Polytech Nantes, France
Imura, Hajime	Hokkaido University, Japan
Ito, Kimihito	Hokkaido University, Japan
Jen, Tao-Yuan	ETIS/University of Cergy Pontoise, France
Kawtrakul, Asanee	Kasetsart University, Thailand
Kritikos, Kyriakos	ICS-FORTH, Greece
Laurent, Dominique	ETIS/University of Cergy Pontoise, France
Lucchese, Claudio	ISTI-CNR, Italy
Marinica, Claudia	ETIS/University of Cergy Pontoise, France
Petit, Jean-Marc	LIRIS/University of Lyon, France

Contents

Information Management

Efficient Identification of the Highest Diversity Gain Object. 3
  Dimitris Sacharidis and Timos Sellis

Dualization on Partially Ordered Sets: Preliminary Results 23
  Lhouari Nourine and Jean Marc Petit

Continuous Top-k Processing of Social Network Information Streams:
A Vision 35
  Abdulhafiz Alkhouli, Dan Vodislav, and Boris Borzic

Information Discovery

Mining Frequent and Homogeneous Closed Itemsets 51
  Ines Hilali, Tao-Yuan Jen, Dominique Laurent, Claudia Marinica,
  and Sadok Ben Yahia

Mining Frequent Itemsets with Vertical Data Layout in MapReduce 66
  Tao-Yuan Jen, Claudia Marinica, and Abir Ghariani

Knowledge Management Applications on the Web and the Cloud

Webble World 3.0: In the Borderland Between Being a
User or a Developer 85
  Micke Kuwahara and Yuzuru Tanaka

Cloud Based Processing Services Based on Linked Data 97
  Elias Grinias and Dimitris Kotzinos

Author Index 113

Information Management

Efficient Identification
of the Highest Diversity Gain Object

Dimitris Sacharidis[1]([⊠]) and Timos Sellis[2]

[1] Technische Universität Wien, Vienna, Austria
`dimitris@ec.tuwien.ac.at`
[2] RMIT University, Melbourne, Australia
`timos.sellis@rmit.edu.au`

Abstract. Diversification has recently attracted a lot of attention, as a means to retrieve objects that are both relevant to a query and sufficiently dissimilar to each other. Since it is a computationally expensive problem, greedy techniques that iteratively identify the most promising objects are typically used. We focus on the sub-task within one iteration and formalize it as the highest diversity gain problem. We show that it is possible to optimally solve such problems, by appropriately defining a novelty function and identifying the object with the highest novelty. Furthermore, we are able to determine parts of the search space than cannot contain promising objects. Based on these results, we propose a greedy diversification algorithm that iteratively invokes a procedure to determine the most novel object. This procedure uses an index to guide the search towards promising objects, and computes bounds to prune large parts of the space. As a result, the procedure is shown to be I/O optimal, under certain conditions, and experimental studies on real and synthetic data demonstrate its efficiency.

1 Introduction

Conventional information retrieval systems return a set of objects that has the highest relevance to a given user query. However, in various situations, such a result set can be of little help to the user, e.g., when the universe of objects is huge and objects contain overlapping or duplicate information, when the query terms are vague and the actual intent of the user is unknown. To increase the usefulness of the result set, a better approach, termed *diversification*, suggests returning objects that are both *relevant* to the query and *diverse*, i.e., dissimilar to each other.

Although they come in various flavors, relevance and diversity generally pose contradictory objectives. The former favors objects similar to the query, while the latter favors objects dissimilar to each other and thus to the query. Therefore, diversification aims to strike a balance between them. In the most common interpretations, the weighted sum of relevance and diversity is defined to be the target optimization function, and the *diversification problem* is stated as finding a set of objects that maximizes this function.

© Springer International Publishing Switzerland 2016
D. Kotzinos et al. (Eds.): ISIP 2014, CCIS 497, pp. 3–22, 2016.
DOI: 10.1007/978-3-319-38901-1_1

Diversification is significantly more expensive than top-k ranking, and it is shown to be NP-hard. Therefore, a simple greedy approach is universally adopted in the literature. Starting with an empty result set, iteratively insert in the set the highest diversity gain object, i.e., the one that maximizes the optimization function computed on the set after the insertion. We segregate the sub-task within one iteration of the greedy approach, and refer to it as the *highest diversity gain problem*.

While there has been an abundance of works on diversification problems, surprisingly little effort has been devoted to studying the highest diversity gain problem. For the majority of works, efficiency is not an issue, and the highest gain object is simply identified after retrieving and exhaustively examining all relevant objects. On the other hand, this work attempts to address this overlooking and aims to attract further attention to the highest diversity gain problem, similarly to recent works in top-k diversification [8,16].

Our work focuses on a broad class of diversification problems, formalizing different definitions of relevance and diversity, computed over sets of attributes, which may or may not overlap. We show that, for this class, it is possible to define a *novelty function* that assigns a score to each object, such that the most novel object is the one with the highest diversity gain. Then, we study this function to gather insight on the possible location of the highest diversity gain object.

Building upon our findings, we propose a simple algorithm, termed DIV, that iteratively invokes the Novelty (NOV) procedure for solving the highest diversity gain problem. NOV utilizes a multidimensional index storing all objects, in order to guide the search towards the most novel object, while avoiding parts of the space that contain unpromising objects. Particularly, NOV computes an upper and lower bound on the novelty of all object within an index node, and makes simple observations to eliminate index subtrees. Therefore, without scanning the entire collection of objects, NOV is able to quickly identify the most novel one. In fact, we show that under certain conditions NOV is *I/O optimal*, i.e., it performs the fewest possible node accesses among any other algorithm that solves the highest diversity gain problem and operates on the same index. Experimental results on real and synthetic data, verify the efficiency of DIV, and show that it is at least an order of magnitude faster than a greedy diversification method [8] and a simple linear scan-based algorithm.

The remainder of this paper is structured as follows. Section 2 reviews related work. Section 3 introduces all concepts and formally states the diversification and highest diversity gain problems. Section 4 presents our approach to the afore-mentioned problems and details the NOV procedure and the DIV algorithm. Section 5 presents our experimental study, and Sect. 6 concludes this paper.

2   Related Work

The need for diversification arises in information retrieval (IR) systems, where for example [3] proposes a reranking approach in order to boost the utility of the search results. Their greedy approach assigns a score to each document, termed *maximal marginal relevance* (MMR), which is used to incrementally retrieve documents. MMR is a weighted combination of relevance and diversity and plays the role of a novelty function (similar to Eq. 2 with the difference that the first term does not consider the diversity of the set $\mathcal{O}$). The authors, however, do not define a global score for a collection of documents, and do not propose any algorithm for finding the MMR.

Subsequent works address different variations of IR diversification. The work of [1] addresses the ambiguity in a user's query, assuming a taxonomy that models the information within queries and documents is available. The relevance of documents is defined with standard metrics, whereas the diversity is computed using the taxonomy. The proposed greedy algorithm returns a set of documents that cover various topics of interest from the taxonomy. In a similar spirit, [19] proposes a method to diversify query results in online shopping applications. In this scenario, the products are classified, and the goal is to design an efficient method to return diverse products with respect to an ordering among the attributes of the classification. To improve result diversification, [5] defines diversity using multiple criteria: anchor texts, query logs, search result clusters and hosts. Their reranking approach defines a composite similarity function over these diversity criteria. The work of [2] targets performance in diversity-aware search. They avoid reranking all relevant documents, by proposing a data access prioritization scheme, in the spirit of [7], that cleverly alternates among five sequential and random access methods.

A useful review of diversification problems is made in [10], where the authors define eight axioms that any diversification system should be expected to satisfy, and prove that no objective function can satisfy all of them. They also make a categorization of common diversification objectives into three classes, MaxSum, MaxMin and mono-objective. The first two classes are related to dispersion problems [11,17], which are shown to be NP-hard. On the other hand, the last class is related to MMR and is easy to process in an incremental manner.

Another study focusing on the performance of various diversification methods, in terms of effectiveness and efficiency, appears in [20]. Their problem formulation is similar to ours, in that they define a global score for a set of objects as the weighted sum of its relevance and diversity. They study local search methods that insert/remove objects from the result set, clustering techniques, as well as algorithms introduced in [3,10]. They also propose two novel algorithms, a probabilistic approach, and a greedy method that progressively inserts the most promising object to the result set, in a manner similar to our framework. However, unlike this work, all these algorithms must examine the entire dataset to determine at each iteration which object to insert or remove from the result set.

Diversification concepts have also appeared in various other domains; see also the survey of [6]. In the context of recommender systems, the goal is to recommend diverse items to the user. The work of [21] measures the diversity among items based on the dissimilarity of their explanations. An item explanation is the set of similar items that the user has highly rated in the past, or the set of similar users that have highly rated this item. Keyword search in structured databases entails constructing a ranked list of structured queries, representing the possible interpretations of the user's intent. The work of [4] uses a probabilistic ranking model that also takes into account the diversity of the query results. In the context of graph databases, [15] finds the top-k diversified "prestige" nodes in information networks using vertex-reinforced random walks. [9] presents a method for diversifying the results of keyword search in graphs.

The diversification problem is closely related to top-k query processing [12]. The work of [13] introduces the k-nearest diverse neighbor problem, whose goal is to return a set of k objects that are as close as possible to a given query point, and at the same time no two objects have diversity below a given threshold. They propose a greedy algorithm that performs a conventional nearest neighbor (NN) search around the query, and iteratively insert the next nearest object if its distance from the current result set is above the threshold. Since it is a variation of the NN problem, the algorithm avoids visiting the entire dataset. However, theirs is a much easier problem that does not apply to our formulation. A similar problem appears in [14], where a query point is specified in a spatial space, and the goal is to maximize an objective function that tradeoffs relevance and diversity. In this setting, relevance is defined as the distance to the query, whereas diversity is defined either as the smallest distance or the angle similarity to an object in the result. The authors propose a greedy incremental method, which however avoids a complete scan of the dataset only for the angle-based diversity. Another related problem is the spatial cohesion query [18], where the goal is to efficiently find the object that balances the attraction to a set of (point or area) attractors and the repulsion from a set of (point or area) repellers. In essence, that problem is a combination of nearest and farthest neighbor search.

The work in [16] defines the problem of top-k diversification as a variation of conventional top-k, adding the restriction that the result set must not contain objects with similarity less than a user defined threshold. Note that this problem definition is similar to [13], but different than ours, as we do not impose a user defined threshold on the diversity of the objects. Another work [8] is more related to our problem formulation, and we discuss it in more detail next.

The SPP Algorithm. The work of [8] assumes objects are embedded in a vector space and solves a problem similar to ours, i.e., their objective function is Eq. 1. The diversity is defined as in this work, but the relevance of an object is given by an unknown function, which is not related to the embedded vector space. In contrast, we define the relevance of an object using the distance of an object to a given query.

Similar to our most novel object approach, the authors apply a greedy approach to the diversification problem by identifying in each iteration the most promising object. For this reason, they define a slightly different than ours (Eq. 2) novelty function. However, this function does not guarantee that they find the best object in each iteration (i.e., Theorem 1 does not hold).

The proposed algorithm, termed SPP, retrieves objects by sorted access according to (1) their relevance, and (2) their distance to any arbitrary probing location in the vector space. The authors show that best probing locations are the vertices of the bounded Voronoi diagram computed on the diversified set of objects found in the previous iterations.

In each SPP iteration, the most promising object is identified. In particular, SPP retrieves multiple objects via sorted access based on either relevance or distance. Among the objects seen, SPP maintains the one with the highest novelty found, and also computes a local upper bound on the novelty of the unseen objects in each probing location. An iteration of SPP terminates when the maximum of these upper bounds is lower than the highest seen novelty.

3 Definitions

Consider a finite set of objects $\mathcal{U}$, termed the universe. An object $\mathbf{o} \in \mathcal{U}$ is defined over a set of numerical attributes $\mathcal{A} = \mathbb{R}^{|\mathcal{A}|}$. We assume that the set of attributes $\mathcal{A}$ is partitioned into two (not necessarily disjoint) sets, $\mathcal{A}^r$ and $\mathcal{A}^v$, defining the relevance and diversity spaces, respectively. We denote as $\mathbf{o}^r$ (resp. $\mathbf{o}^v$) the projection of the object $\mathbf{o}$ in the relevance (resp. diversity) space.

Given a query $\mathbf{q}$ defined in the relevance space, the *relevance* of an object $\mathbf{o}$ is the opposite of Euclidean distance between the projection of the object in the relevance space and $\mathbf{q}$, i.e., $rel(\mathbf{o}|\mathbf{q}) = -d(\mathbf{o}^r, \mathbf{q}) = -\|\mathbf{o}^r - \mathbf{q}\|_2$. The smaller the distance of an object from $\mathbf{q}$, the greater its relevance.

The *diversity* of two objects $\mathbf{o}_1, \mathbf{o}_2$ is the Euclidean distance between their projections in the diversity space, i.e., $div(\mathbf{o}_1, \mathbf{o}_2) = d(\mathbf{o}_1^v, \mathbf{o}_2^v) = \|\mathbf{o}_1^v - \mathbf{o}_2^v\|_2$. The larger the distance between two objects, the greater their diversity.

The aforementioned definitions can be extended to the case of a set of objects. Given a query $\mathbf{q}$, the relevance of a set of objects $\mathcal{O} \subseteq \mathcal{U}$ is defined as:

$$rel(\mathcal{O}|\mathbf{q}) = \sum_{\mathbf{o} \in \mathcal{O}} rel(\mathbf{o}|\mathbf{q}) = - \sum_{\mathbf{o} \in \mathcal{O}} d(\mathbf{o}^r, \mathbf{q}).$$

The diversity of a set of objects $\mathcal{O}$ is defined as:

$$div(\mathcal{O}) = \min_{\mathbf{o}_i \neq \mathbf{o}_j \in \mathcal{O}} div(\mathbf{o}_i, \mathbf{o}_j) = \min_{\mathbf{o}_i \neq \mathbf{o}_j \in \mathcal{O}} d(\mathbf{o}_i^v, \mathbf{o}_j^v).$$

Given a query $\mathbf{q}$, the *score* of a set of objects $\mathcal{O}$ is the weighted sum of the set's diversity and relevance, i.e.,

$$s(\mathcal{O}|\mathbf{q}) = \alpha \cdot div(\mathcal{O}) + \beta \cdot rel(\mathcal{O}|\mathbf{q})$$
$$= \alpha \cdot \min_{\mathbf{o}_i \neq \mathbf{o}_j \in \mathcal{O}} div(\mathbf{o}_i, \mathbf{o}_j) + \beta \cdot \sum_{\mathbf{o} \in \mathcal{O}} rel(\mathbf{o}|\mathbf{q}). \qquad (1)$$

Note that the values α, β should not only reflect the relative weight between diversity and relevance, but also account for normalization (e.g., in this formulation relevance is the sum of $|\mathcal{O}|$ distances, whereas diversity is a single distance). In the remainder of this paper, we set $\alpha = \beta = 1$ to aid readability. All formulas and algorithms can be trivially extended to arbitrary weight values. Therefore, the score of $\mathcal{O}$ is defined as:

$$s(\mathcal{O}|\mathbf{q}) = \min_{\mathbf{o}_i \neq \mathbf{o}_j \in \mathcal{O}} d(\mathbf{o}_i^v, \mathbf{o}_j^v) - \sum_{o \in \mathcal{O}} d(\mathbf{o}^r, \mathbf{q}).$$

We next formalize the diversification and highest diversity gain problems. Note that given a set of objects $\mathcal{O} \subseteq \mathcal{U}$, the notation $\mathbf{o} \notin \mathcal{O}$ refers to an object $\mathbf{o} \in \mathcal{U} \setminus \mathcal{O}$.

Problem 1 [k-Diversification]. Find a set $\mathcal{O}_k^* \subseteq \mathcal{U}$ of k objects with the highest score among all other sets of equal size, i.e.,

$$\mathcal{O}_k^* = \operatorname*{argmax}_{\mathcal{O}_k \subseteq \mathcal{U}, |\mathcal{O}_k| = k} s(\mathcal{O}_k|\mathbf{q}).$$

Problem 2 [Highest Diversity Gain]. Given a query $\mathbf{q}$ and a set of objects $\mathcal{O}$, find an object $\mathbf{o}^* \notin \mathcal{O}$ such that the set $\mathcal{O} \cup \{\mathbf{o}^*\}$ has the greatest score, i.e.,

$$\mathbf{o}^* = \operatorname*{argmax}_{\mathbf{o} \notin \mathcal{O}} s(\mathcal{O} \cup \{\mathbf{o}\}|\mathbf{q}).$$

The object $\mathbf{o}^*$ is called the *highest diversity gain object*, with respect to $\mathcal{O}$ and $\mathbf{q}$. Note that it is possible that more than one objects maximize the score; to simplify presentation, we assume that $\mathbf{o}^*$ is any of them.

A well-known greedy approach, followed by several works (e.g. [3,8,10]), for solving the k-diversification problem is to solve k instances of the highest diversity gain problem as follows. Define a sequence of sets of objects $\{\mathcal{O}_i\}$, for $0 \leq i \leq k$. The first term $\mathcal{O}_0$ is the empty set. Then, the i-th term $\mathcal{O}_i$ includes the $(i-1)$-th term $\mathcal{O}_{i-1}$ and the highest diversity gain object with respect to $\mathcal{O}_{i-1}$ and $\mathbf{q}$, i.e., $\mathcal{O}_i = \mathcal{O}_{i-1} \cup \{\mathbf{o}_i^*\}$.

4   Methodology

We present our methodology for solving the highest gain and diversification problem. Section 4.1 introduces the novelty function and Sect. 4.2 presents important observations for eliminating unpromising objects. Then, Sects. 4.3 and 4.4 describe the algorithms for solving the two problems. Section 4.5 discusses the case of nonidentical relevance and diversity spaces. Table 1 gathers the most important symbols used throughout this paper.

4.1   The Novelty Function

Given a query $\mathbf{q}$, a set of objects $\mathcal{O}$, we define the *novelty* of an object $\mathbf{o} \notin \mathcal{O}$ as:

$$n(\mathbf{o}|\mathcal{O}, \mathbf{q}) = \min\{div(\mathcal{O}), \min_{\mathbf{o}' \in \mathcal{O}} d(\mathbf{o}^v, \mathbf{o}'^v)\} + rel(\mathbf{o}|\mathbf{q}). \qquad (2)$$

The following theorem shows the importance of the novelty function. It implies that to solve the highest gain problem, it suffices to find the *most novel object*, i.e., the one with the largest novelty.

Table 1. Notation

Symbol	Definition
$\mathcal{U}$	universe of objects
$\mathcal{A}$, $\mathcal{A}^r$, $\mathcal{A}^v$	set of all, relevance, diversity attributes
$\mathbf{o}$	an object
$\mathbf{q}$	the query
$d(\mathbf{x}, \mathbf{y})$	Euclidean distance ($\|\mathbf{x} - \mathbf{y}\|_2$)
$rel(\mathbf{o}|\mathbf{q})$	relevance of $\mathbf{o}$ w.r.t. $\mathbf{q}$
$div(\mathbf{o}_1, \mathbf{o}_2)$	diversity of $\mathbf{o}_1$ and $\mathbf{o}_2$
$\mathcal{O}$	a set of objects
$rel(\mathcal{O}|\mathbf{q})$	relevance of $\mathcal{O}$ w.r.t. $\mathbf{q}$
$div(\mathcal{O})$	diversity of $\mathcal{O}$
$s(\mathcal{O}|\mathbf{q})$	score of $\mathcal{O}$ w.r.t. $\mathbf{q}$
$n(\mathbf{o}|\mathcal{O}, \mathbf{q})$	novelty of $\mathbf{o}$ w.r.t. $\mathcal{O}$ and $\mathbf{q}$
δ	diversity of $\mathcal{O}$ w.r.t. $\mathbf{q}$
τ	a novelty value
$\mathbf{o}_{NN}$	nearest neighbor of $\mathbf{o} \notin \mathcal{O}$ in $\mathcal{O}$
T, N	R*-Tree indexing the universe, a node of T
$n^+(N)$, $n^-(N)$	upper, lower bound of novelty of objects in N

Theorem 1. *The most novel object is the highest gain object, i.e., for any object* $\mathbf{o} \notin \mathcal{O}$ *the following holds* $\mathbf{o}^* = argmax\, n(\mathbf{o}|\mathcal{O}, \mathbf{q}) = argmax\, s(\mathcal{O} \cup \{\mathbf{o}\}|\mathbf{q})$.

Proof. We prove by contradiction. Let $\mathbf{o}^n \neq \mathbf{o}^*$ be the object that has the largest novelty, so that $n(\mathbf{o}^*|\mathcal{O}, \mathbf{q}) < n(\mathbf{o}^n|\mathcal{O}, \mathbf{q})$.

Consider the score of the set $\mathcal{O} \cup \{\mathbf{o}^*\}$ and observe that:

$$s(\mathcal{O} \cup \{\mathbf{o}^*\}) = \min \left\{ \min_{\mathbf{o}_i \neq \mathbf{o}_j \in \mathcal{O}} d(\mathbf{o}_i^v, \mathbf{o}_j^v), \min_{\mathbf{o}' \in \mathcal{O}} d(\mathbf{o}^{*v}, \mathbf{o}'^v) \right\}$$

$$- \left(\sum_{\mathbf{o} \in \mathcal{O}} d(\mathbf{o}^r, \mathbf{q}) + d(\mathbf{o}^{*r}, \mathbf{q}) \right)$$

$$= n(\mathbf{o}^*|\mathcal{O}, \mathbf{q}) - \sum_{\mathbf{o} \in \mathcal{O}} d(\mathbf{o}^r, \mathbf{q}).$$

Similarly, when the object $\mathbf{o}^n$ is included:

$$s(\mathcal{O} \cup \{\mathbf{o}^n\}) = n(\mathbf{o}^n|\mathcal{O}, \mathbf{q}) - \sum_{\mathbf{o} \in \mathcal{O}} d(\mathbf{o}^r, \mathbf{q}).$$

Since $n(\mathbf{o}^*|\mathcal{O}, \mathbf{q}) < n(\mathbf{o}^n|\mathcal{O}, \mathbf{q})$, we obtain that $s(\mathcal{O} \cup \{\mathbf{o}^*\}) < s(\mathcal{O} \cup \{\mathbf{o}^n\})$, which is a contradiction as $\mathbf{o}^*$ maximizes the score. $\square$

4.2   Observations

Over the next sections, we assume that diversity and relevance are defined over the same space, i.e., $\mathcal{A}^r = \mathcal{A}^v = \mathcal{A}$. Therefore, we drop all r and v superscripts. Later, in Sect. 4.5, we lift this restriction. Also note that for illustration purposes, all examples assume that $\mathcal{A} = \mathbb{R}^2$, i.e., the Euclidean plane.

Moreover, we simplify notation by introducing the following concepts. We denote by δ the diversity of the set $\mathcal{O}$, i.e., $\delta = div(\mathcal{O})$. Given an object $\mathbf{o}$, we define $\mathbf{o}_{NN}$ to be its nearest neighbor within $\mathcal{O}$, i.e., $\mathbf{o}_{NN} = \operatorname{argmin}_{\mathbf{o}' \in \mathcal{O}} d(\mathbf{o}, \mathbf{o}')$. Since the set $\mathcal{O}$ and query $\mathbf{q}$ are fixed, we drop the $\mathcal{O}, \mathbf{q}$ designation for the novelty of an object $\mathbf{o}$, and thus Eq. 2 simplifies to:

$$n(\mathbf{o}) = \min\{\delta, d(\mathbf{o}, \mathbf{o}_{NN})\} - d(\mathbf{o}, \mathbf{q}). \tag{3}$$

We present two observations for eliminating objects that have novelty less than a known value.

Observation 1. *Given a set of objects $\mathcal{O}$, a query $\mathbf{q}$, and a known novelty value τ, any object $\mathbf{o} \notin \mathcal{O}$ such that $d(\mathbf{o}, \mathbf{q}) > \delta - \tau$ has novelty less than τ.*

Proof. The novelty of an object $\mathbf{o}$ satisfying this criterion is $n(\mathbf{o}) = \min\{\delta, d(\mathbf{o}, \mathbf{o}_{NN})\} - d(\mathbf{o}, \mathbf{q}) < \min\{\delta, d(\mathbf{o}, \mathbf{o}_{NN})\} + \tau - \delta$. Since $\delta \geq \min\{\delta, d(\mathbf{o}, \mathbf{o}_{NN})\}$, we obtain $n(\mathbf{o}) < \tau$.   □

Observation 2. *Given a set of objects $\mathcal{O}$, a query $\mathbf{q}$, an object $\mathbf{o}' \in \mathcal{O}$ and a novelty value τ, any object $\mathbf{o} \notin \mathcal{O}$ such that $d(\mathbf{o}, \mathbf{o}') - d(\mathbf{o}, \mathbf{q}) < \tau$ has novelty less than τ.*

Proof. For any object $\mathbf{o} \notin \mathcal{O}$ and its nearest neighbor $\mathbf{o}_{NN}$ within $\mathcal{O}$, it holds that $d(\mathbf{o}, \mathbf{o}') \geq d(\mathbf{o}, \mathbf{o}_{NN})$. Moreover, since $d(\mathbf{o}, \mathbf{o}_{NN}) \geq \min\{\delta, d(\mathbf{o}, \mathbf{o}_{NN})\}$, the novelty of object $\mathbf{o}$ is $n(\mathbf{o}) \leq d(\mathbf{o}, \mathbf{o}') - d(\mathbf{o}, \mathbf{q})$. Therefore, any object $\mathbf{o}$ satisfying the criterion must have $n(\mathbf{o}) < \tau$.   □

Note that Observation 2 holds, and is in fact stronger, when we substitute $\mathbf{o}'$ with $\mathbf{o}$'s nearest neighbor $\mathbf{o}_{NN}$ within $\mathcal{O}$.

4.3   Finding the Most Novel Object

This section introduces the *Novelty* (NOV) procedure for solving the highest gain problem. The key idea is to use an index in order to direct the search towards the most promising object while pruning groups of unpromising objects.

We build an R*-Tree T on the Euclidean space $\mathcal{A}$ indexing the universe of objects $\mathcal{U}$. Each node N corresponds to a disk page, is associated with a rectangle $N.mbr$, and contains a number of child nodes. A leaf node N represents an object $\mathbf{o}$, and thus its rectangle is the point in $\mathcal{A}$ corresponding to this object. The rectangle of an internal node N is the minimum bounding rectangle (MBR) of (i.e., the smallest rectangle that encloses) all children rectangles.

We say that an object o is in a node N, denoted as $o \in N$, if o is represented by a leaf node in the subtree rooted at N. Furthermore, given a point x, we define $\mathtt{mindist}(N, x)$ (resp. $\mathtt{maxdist}(N, x)$) to be the smallest (resp. largest) possible distance to x of any point within the MBR of N.

In the following, we present a set of observations regarding the novelty of objects in a given non-leaf node.

Novelty Bounds. Given a non-leaf node N, but not the objects within its subtree, it is possible to compute bounds on the novelty of any object in N.

Lemma 1. *Given a set of objects $\mathcal{O}$ and a non-leaf node N, the novelty of an object o in N cannot be more than $n^+(N) = \delta - \mathtt{mindist}(N, q)$ if $|\mathcal{O}| > 1$, and cannot be more than $n^+(N) = \mathtt{maxdist}(N, o') - \mathtt{mindist}(N, q)$ if $\mathcal{O} = \{o'\}$.*

Proof. Assume $|\mathcal{O}| > 1$, when δ is defined. Clearly, for any object $o \in N$ it holds that $\delta \geq \min\{\delta, d(o, o_{NN})\}$. By the definition of $\mathtt{mindist}$ and since any object $o \in N$ lies within $N.mbr$, we have $\mathtt{mindist}(N, q) \leq d(o, q)$. Combining the two inequalities, we derive $n^+(N) \geq n(o)$ for any object $o \in N$ and $|\mathcal{O}| > 1$.

Assume $\mathcal{O} = \{o'\}$. By the definition of $\mathtt{maxdist}$ and since any object $o \in N$ is within $N.mbr$, we have $\mathtt{maxdist}(N, o') \leq d(o, o')$. Also, we have $\mathtt{mindist}(N, q) \leq d(o, q)$. Combining the two inequalities, we derive $n^+(N) \geq n(o)$ for any object $o \in N$ and $\mathcal{O} = \{o'\}$. □

Lemma 1 implies that the non-leaf node with the highest $n^+()$ value is more likely to contain the most novel object, and thus provides the means to direct the search.

Lemma 2. *Given a set of objects $\mathcal{O}$ and a non-leaf node N, the novelty of an object o in N cannot be less than $n^-(N) = -\mathtt{maxdist}(N, q)$.*

Proof. For any object $o \in N$ it holds that $\min\{\delta, d(o, o_{NN})\} \geq 0$ and $d(o, q) \leq \mathtt{maxdist}(N, q)$. Therefore, its novelty is $n(o) \geq -\mathtt{maxdist}(N, q)$. □

Lemma 2 provides a lower bound on the novelty of the most novel object: $n(o^*) \geq n^-(N)$ for any non-leaf node N.

Applying Observation 1. The following lemma applies Observation 1 for a node N.

Lemma 3. *Given a novelty value τ, a node N contains objects with novelty less than τ, if $\mathtt{mindist}(N, q) > \delta - \tau$.*

Proof. Any object $o \in N$ has $d(o, q) \geq \mathtt{mindist}(N, q)$. From the condition of the lemma, we obtain $d(o, q) > \delta - \tau$. Thus, Observation 1 applies for all objects $o \in N$. □

Applying Observation 2. The following lemmas apply Observation 2 for a node N.

Lemma 4. *Given a novelty value τ, a node N contains objects with novelty less than τ, if there exists an object $\mathbf{o}' \in \mathcal{O}$ such that $\mathtt{maxdist}(N, \mathbf{o}') - \mathtt{mindist}(N, \mathbf{q}) < \tau$.*

Proof. For any object $\mathbf{o} \in N$ the following conditions hold: $d(\mathbf{o}, \mathbf{o}') \leq \mathtt{maxdist}(N, \mathbf{o}')$ and $d(\mathbf{o}, \mathbf{q}) \geq \mathtt{mindist}(N, \mathbf{q})$. It also holds that $d(\mathbf{o}, \mathbf{o}') - d(\mathbf{o}, \mathbf{q}) < \tau$ and thus Observation 2 applies for all objects within N. $\qquad\square$

Algorithm Description. Algorithm 1 presents the pseudocode of the NOV procedure. NOV takes as input the R*-Tree T indexing all objects in the universe, the query q, and the set of objects $\mathcal{O}$, and returns the most novel object $\mathbf{o}^*$ with respect to $\mathcal{O}$ and $\mathbf{q}$.

NOV maintains a novelty value τ, initially set to $-\infty$, which corresponds to a lower bound of the highest possible novelty. It also computes the diversity of $\mathcal{O}$ and initializes H (line 1). NOV directs the search using the heap H, which contains nodes sorted descending on their novelty upper bound (Lemma 1).

NOV performs a number of iterations (lines 3–15), where at the end of each iteration the node N_x at the top of the heap is popped (line 15); for the first iteration N_x is the root node of T (line 2). NOV terminates when node N_x is a leaf, in which case the object corresponding to this node is the most novel object $\mathbf{o}^*$ (line 16).

Assuming that N_x is not a leaf, NOV reads this node from disk (line 4) and checks if Lemmas 3 and 4 apply for its children (lines 5–14). Particularly, it first checks if Lemma 3 applies for a child N (lines 7–8). If not, NOV examines all objects within the set $\mathcal{O}$ (lines 9–11). For each such object $\mathbf{o}'$, the algorithm checks if Lemma 4 (lines 10–11) applies for node N. If neither lemma applies (lines 12–14), then N is pushed in the heap (line 14), and the novelty value is appropriately updated (line 13) according to Lemma 2.

Correctness and Optimality. The next theorems prove the correctness and I/O optimality of NOV.

Theorem 2. *The NOV procedure returns the most novel object.*

Proof. We show that NOV cannot miss the most novel object $\mathbf{o}^*$. NOV prunes nodes of the R*-Tree based on Lemmas 2–4. Therefore, by the correctness of these lemmas, $\mathbf{o}^*$ cannot be in any pruned node.

NOV terminates when it pops from the heap a leaf corresponding to object $\mathbf{o}_x$. Since the heap contains nodes sorted by the upper bound of Lemma 1, it holds that $n(\mathbf{o}_x) \geq n^+(N)$ for all nodes $N \in H$. By the correctness of the lemma, $\mathbf{o}_x$ has higher novelty than any object within any of the nodes in the heap. $\quad\square$

Intuitively, I/O optimality means that an R*-Tree-based algorithm only visits nodes that *may contain* the most novel object. To formalize this, we introduce the notion of the search frontier.

Given the most novel object $\mathbf{o}^*$, define the *search frontier* (SF) to be the part of the space that contains points with novelty more than $n(\mathbf{o}^*)$. Since $\mathbf{o}^*$ has the highest possible novelty among objects in $\mathcal{U} \setminus \mathcal{O}$, the SF contains no object.

Algorithm 1. NOV

Input: R*-Tree T; objects $\mathcal{O}$; query $\mathbf{q}$
Output: $\mathbf{o}^*$ the most novel object
Variables: H a heap with nodes sorted by $n^+()$; novelty value τ

1   $\tau \leftarrow -\infty$; $\delta \leftarrow div(\mathcal{O})$; $H \leftarrow \varnothing$
2   $N_x \leftarrow N_{root}$ $\triangleright$ root node of T
3   **while** N_x *is non-leaf* **do**
4   read node N_x
5   **foreach** *child* N *of* N_x **do**
6         $pruned \leftarrow false$
7   **if** $\texttt{mindist}(N, \mathbf{q}) > \delta - \tau$ **then** $\triangleright$ Lemma 3
8            $pruned \leftarrow true$
9   **foreach** $\mathbf{o}' \in \mathcal{O}$ **do**
10   **if** $\texttt{maxdist}(N, \mathbf{o}') - \texttt{mindist}(N, \mathbf{q}) < \tau$ **then** $\triangleright$ Lemma 4
11             $pruned \leftarrow true$
12   **if** *not pruned* **then**
13   **if** $n^-(N) > \tau$ **then** $\tau \leftarrow n^-(N)$ $\triangleright$ Lemma 2
14           $\texttt{push}(H, N)$
15      $N_x \leftarrow \texttt{pop}(H)$
16 $\mathbf{o}^* \leftarrow N_x.mbr$

However, it holds that any R*-Tree-based algorithm, which finds the most novel object, must access all nodes that intersect the SF. This is true even for a node N that does not contain $\mathbf{o}^*$; the reason is that the algorithm cannot determine this containment unless it retrieves the contents of N.

Therefore, I/O optimality means that an algorithm only accesses nodes that intersect with the SF, and never visits the same node twice.

To prove I/O optimality for NOV, we must ensure that the upper bound on the novelty of a node is *tight*. In other words, there must exist a point within the node's MBB (not necessarily an object in $\mathcal{U}$) such that its novelty is equal to the upper bound. The upper bound of Lemma 1 is not tight. However, given a node it is possible to compute a tight upper bound in an analytical way. The key idea is to find a point within the node's MBB that maximizes the novelty function. This point must be one of the critical points where all partial derivatives of the novelty function become zero.

Theorem 3. *The NOV procedure with a tight upper bound on novelty is I/O optimal.*

Proof. First, NOV never visits the same node twice. The reason is that a node is only inserted once in the heap, and NOV always removes from the heap the node it visits.

We next prove that NOV with a tight upper bound on novelty $n^+()$ never accesses a node that does not intersect with the SF, defined by the most novel

---

Algorithm 2. DIV

Input: R*-Tree T; query $\mathbf{q}$
Output: $\mathcal{O}$ the k-diversified set of objects
Variables: $\mathbf{o}^*$ current most novel object

1 $\mathcal{O} \leftarrow \varnothing$
2 **for** $i \leftarrow 1$ **to** k **do**
3      $\mathbf{o}^* \leftarrow \text{NOV}(T, \mathcal{O}, \mathbf{q})$
4      $\mathcal{O} \leftarrow \mathcal{O} \cup \{\mathbf{o}^*\}$

---

object $\mathbf{o}^*$. Assume the contrary, i.e., that NOV visits a node N that does not intersect with the SF. Since N is outside the SF, for any point (not necessarily an object in $\mathcal{U}$) $\mathbf{p} \in N$ it holds that $n(\mathbf{p}) < n(\mathbf{o}^*)$. By the property of the tight upper bound, there exists a point $\mathbf{p}' \in N$ such that $n(\mathbf{p}') = n^+(N)$. Moreover, since N is visited it must hold that $n^+(N) > n(\mathbf{o}^*)$. Therefore, $n(\mathbf{p}') > n(\mathbf{o}^*)$, which contradicts the fact that N is outside the SF. $\qquad\square$

4.4   Solving the Diversification Problem

We next present a simple algorithm, termed DIV, that solves the k-diversification problem by invoking k times the NOV procedure. Algorithm 2 shows the pseudocode of DIV. The algorithm takes as input the R*-Tree T indexing all objects in the universe, the query $\mathbf{q}$, and returns the k-diversified set of objects $\mathcal{O}$.

DIV initializes the set of diversified objects $\mathcal{O}$ to be empty (line 1). Then it calls k times the NOV procedure (lines 2–4). In each invocation, DIV obtains the next most novel object $\mathbf{o}^*$ (line 3) and inserts it into the set $\mathcal{O}$ (line 4).

4.5   Generalization for Nonidentical Relevance and Diversity Spaces

So far, we have assumed that relevance and diversity are defined over the same set of attributes. This section discusses the general case when $\mathcal{A}^r \subseteq \mathcal{A}$ and $\mathcal{A}^v \subseteq \mathcal{A}$. Note that the query $\mathbf{q}$ takes values only for the relevance attributes $\mathcal{A}^r$, while an object $\mathbf{o}$ takes values on all attributes. To illustrate the concepts, we assume a three-dimensional example where $\mathcal{A}^r = \{A_1, A_2\}$ and $\mathcal{A}^v = \{A_2, A_3\}$.

We define the *extension* of the query $\mathbf{q}$, denoted by $\rho(\mathbf{q})$, as the set of points in $\mathcal{A}$ such that $\rho(\mathbf{q}).A_x = \mathbf{q}.A_x$, for all $A_x \in \mathcal{A}^r$, and $\rho(\mathbf{q}).A_y = [-\infty, +\infty]$, for all $A_y \notin \mathcal{A}^r$. The extension has the property that for any object $\mathbf{o} \in \mathcal{U}$, it holds that $rel(\mathbf{o}|\mathbf{q}) = -d(\mathbf{o}^r, \mathbf{q}) = -d(\mathbf{o}, \rho(\mathbf{q}))$, i.e., the relevance of $\mathbf{o}$ is given by the distance between $\rho(\mathbf{q})$ and $\mathbf{o}$ computed *over all attributes*. In our three-dimensional example, $\rho(\mathbf{q})$ represents a line perpendicular to the A_1, A_2 plane, and the relevance of $\mathbf{o}$ is its (perpendicular) distance to this line.

Similarly, we define the *restriction* of an object $\mathbf{o}$, denoted by $\pi(\mathbf{o})$, as the set of points in $\mathcal{A}$ such that $\pi(\mathbf{o}).A_x = \mathbf{o}.A_x$, for all $A_x \in \mathcal{A}^v$, and $\pi(\mathbf{o}).A_y = [-\infty, +\infty]$, for all $A_y \notin \mathcal{A}^v$. The extension has the property that for any other object $\mathbf{o}' \in \mathcal{U}$, it holds that $div(\mathbf{o}', \mathbf{o}) = d(\mathbf{o}'^v, \mathbf{o}^v) = d(\mathbf{o}', \pi(\mathbf{o}))$, i.e., the diversity of $\mathbf{o}'$ and $\mathbf{o}$ is given by the distance between $\mathbf{o}'$ and the restriction of $\mathbf{o}$ computed *over all attributes*. In our three-dimensional example, $\pi(\mathbf{o})$ represents a line perpendicular to the A_2, A_3 plane, and the diversity of $\mathbf{o}$ and another object $\mathbf{o}'$ is the (perpendicular) distance of $\mathbf{o}'$ to this line.

Using the previous transformations and in analogy to Eq. 3, the novelty of an object $\mathbf{o}$ becomes

$$n(\mathbf{o}) = \min\{\delta, d(\mathbf{o}, \pi(\mathbf{o}_{NN}))\} - d(\mathbf{o}, \rho(\mathbf{q})).$$

More importantly, the two main results of Sect. 4.2 hold, if we substitute $\mathbf{q}$ with $\rho(\mathbf{q})$ and $\mathbf{o}'$ with $\pi(\mathbf{o}')$. Given the aforementioned transformations, adapting NOV is straightforward. Observe that all Lemmas 1–4 hold, as long as we substitute $\mathbf{q}$ with $\rho(\mathbf{q})$ and $\mathbf{o}'$ with $\pi(\mathbf{o}')$.

5   Experimental Evaluation

Section 5.1 describes the setting, while Sect. 5.2 contains the results.

5.1   Setting

Methods. We implement our proposed diversification method DIV, which is based on the NOV procedure. We also implement the SPP algorithm from [8], and adapt it to consider at each iteration the same novelty function with DIV. Recall that SPP requires a module that provides sorted access on the universe of objects based on their distance from a given location. In our implementation, this module performs nearest neighbor search using the same R*-Tree as in DIV. Furthermore, as a baseline, we implement a greedy algorithm denoted as LIN. In each iteration, LIN performs an exhaustive linear scan over the universe of objects to identify the most novel one, and inserts it into the result set. All algorithms are implemented in C++ and executed on a 2 GHz machine, whose disk page size is 4096 bytes.

Datasets. We use a real and two synthetic datasets in our evaluation. The real dataset[1], denoted as NE, is a two-dimensional collection of 125,000 postal addresses in three metropolitan areas, New York, Philadelphia and Boston. The synthetic dataset UNI contains independent and uniformly distributed random objects. The synthetic dataset CLU contains objects that are randomly distributed around 1,000 cluster centers. The probability with which a cluster center attracts objects is drawn from a Zipfian distribution with degree 0.8.

Parameters and Metrics. We study the effect on the performance of the algorithms of three parameters: number of objects in the universe, number of attributes and value of k. Particularly, for the NE dataset, the number of objects is fixed to $|\mathcal{U}| = 125K$ and the dimensionality to $|\mathcal{A}| = 2$. Table 2 shows the

---

[1] Available at http://www.rtreeportal.org.

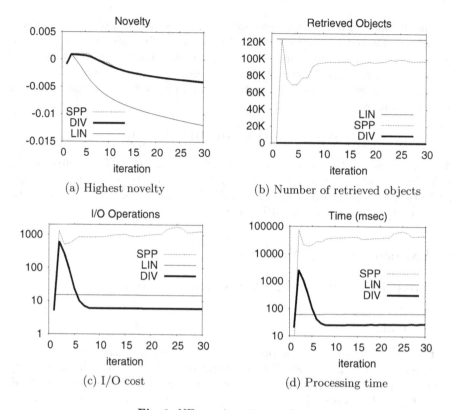

Fig. 1. NE, per iteration analysis

range of values examined for each parameter. In each experiment, we vary a single parameter and set the others to their default values.

To quantify performance, we measure the number of retrieved objects, the number of I/O operations, and the total processing time. The reported values are the averages of 10 distinct executions with queries uniformly selected at random from the space. We emphasize that the objective of this work is to improve the efficiency of solving the diversification problem, and not on the quality of the constructed result set. In fact, all implemented methods follow the same iterative heuristic and thus construct the same result set (save for differences due to ties) with identical global scores.

Table 2. Parameters

Symbol	Values	Default
$|\mathcal{U}|$	100K, 500K, 1M, 5M, 10M	1M
$|\mathcal{A}|$	2, 3, 4, 5, 6	2
k	[1, 50]	20

5.2   Results

Per Iteration Analysis. In the first experiment, we study the performance of all algorithms as they iteratively find promising objects. For this setting, we use the NE dataset and set $k = 30$. Figure 1 contains the results, where the bold, regular, dotted line corresponds to DIV, LIN, SPP, respectively.

Figure 1a depicts the novelty value of the most novel object found at each iteration. Observe that at the first iteration, all methods select the nearest neighbor to the query whose novelty is equal to minus the distance to the query. At the second iteration, all methods select objects that have the same novelty. However, these two initial objects may differ among methods, depending on how they solve ties in novelty. In fact after this point, at each iteration, the selection of the object among those with equal novelty may affects the best novelty values in subsequent iterations. This phenomenon is observed in Fig. 1a, where the novelty graphs vary slightly between DIV and SPP, and a bit more with respect to LIN. The fact that LIN's highest novelty is significantly lower is attributed to unfortunate choices when breaking ties. Note that the highest novelty of all methods decreases because the relevance term of the novelty function dominates the diversity one, while objects farther from the query are inserted.

Figure 1b shows the number of objects retrieved at each iteration. LIN needs to scan the entire dataset at each iteration, hence it performs the maximum number of retrievals (125K). On the other hand, DIV always guides search towards the most novel object, and thus performs a single retrieval at each iteration. SPP performs a single retrieval in the first iteration to identify the nearest to the query object. However, at all other iterations, SPP must examine a very large set of objects. Even though SPP prunes the search space, it cannot guide the search towards the non-pruned space. The main reason is that the set of probing locations remains fixed throughout an iteration.

Figure 1c shows the number of I/O operations performed at each iteration. LIN retrieves constantly 16 pages from disk. DIV performs 5 I/Os to retrieve the first object and constantly 6 I/Os to retrieve objects after the seventh iteration. For iterations 2 and 3 DIV requires more than 100 I/Os to retrieve the most novel object. The reason is that, in the beginning, the set of retrieved objects is too small to prune large parts of the space. Regarding SPP, note that except in the first iteration, it performs I/Os in the order of 1,000. There are two reasons for this. SPP needs to retrieve a large number of objects (although less than LIN), and each retrieval may cost up to 5 I/Os due to the nearest neighbor search. To make matters worse, since SPP initiates multiple NN searches at different probing locations, it happens that the same object is retrieved at more than one NN search. This last reason explains why the number of I/Os increases at each iteration: the number of probing locations also increases.

Figure 1d shows the processing time per iteration. LIN require constant time, around 60 msec, per iteration. The same holds for DIV after the seventh iteration, as it requires around 25 msec, per iteration. On the other hand SPP requires more than 10 s for each iteration after the first.

Per Iteration Analysis with Fixed $\mathcal{O}$. We repeat the first experiment, but at this time we force DIV and LIN to start each iteration with the same set of objects as SPP. In other words, for fairness at each iteration, all algorithms solve an identical instance of the highest diversity gain problem. The lines for LIN and SPP are not affected in this experiment. The number of I/O operations and the per iteration processing time of DIV are largely unaffected by the enforcement of common $\mathcal{O}$ accross methods (Fig. 2).

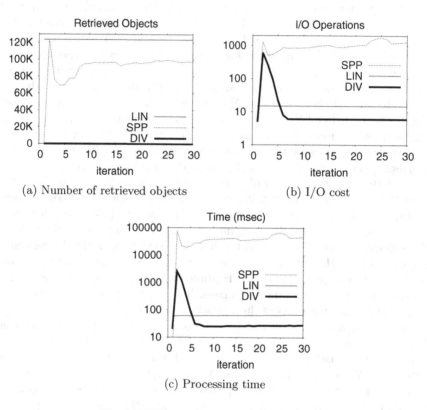

(a) Number of retrieved objects

(b) I/O cost

(c) Processing time

Fig. 2. NE, per iteration analysis, fixed $\mathcal{O}$

In the remainder of the experimental evaluation, we exclude the SPP algorithm due to its high processing cost.

Effect of k. In the next experiment, we vary the k value from 1 up to 50 in increments of one, while we set the number of objects fixed to $|\mathcal{U}| = 1M$. Figure 3 plots the results as a function of k. Note that in contrast to the previous experiments, the reported times are at the end of the algorithms execution and not per iteration.

Figure 3a shows the I/O cost of LIN and DIV for the CLU dataset. Observe that the I/O cost of LIN grows linearly with k, since the cost per iteration is constant (see the discussion in the context of Fig. 1). Note that the I/O cost of

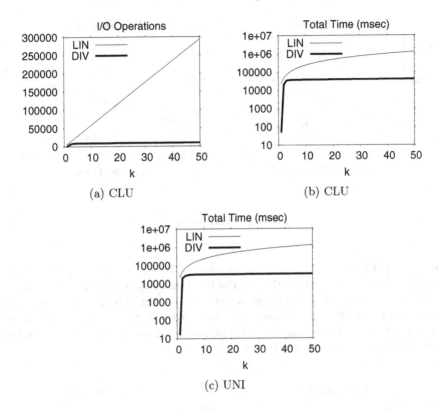

Fig. 3. Effect of k

DIV for $k = 1$ is minimal, and that it slightly grows with k, so little that the trend is not apparent in the figure. This is in accordance to our per iteration analysis, where DIV's cost for retrieving additional objects is minor.

Figure 3b depicts the total processing time for the CLU dataset. Note that processing time is shown on a logarithmic axis. The trends that appear in the previous figure, also show here. DIV is already more than an order of magnitude faster than LIN for $k = 20$ and the gap increases with k. Figure 3c presents the effect of k on processing time for the UNI dataset. The trends are identical to those for the CLU dataset.

Varing $|\mathcal{U}|$. In this experiment, we vary the number of object in the universe $|\mathcal{U}|$ from $100\,\mathrm{K}$ up to 10M, while we set $k = 20$. Figure 4 depicts the total processing time as a function of $|\mathcal{U}|$.

Figure 4a shows the processing time of DIV and LIN on the CLU dataset. As the number of objects increases, it becomes harder to identify the k object with the highest novelty. Hence the performance of both methods decreases with $|\mathcal{U}|$. Observe, however that the benefit of DIV over LIN remains constant at more than one order of magnitude. Similar results hold for the UNI dataset, as shown in Fig. 4b.

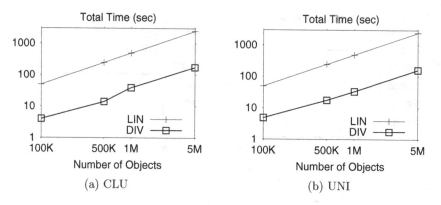

Fig. 4. Effect of $|\mathcal{U}|$

Varing $|\mathcal{A}|$. Finally, we increase the number of attributes $|\mathcal{A}|$, i.e., dimensionality, from 2 up to 6. Figure 5 depicts the total processing time as a function of $|\mathcal{A}|$. Figure 5a shows that the performance of both methods deteriorates as the dimensionality of the CLU dataset increases. Note that the relative benefit of DIV against LIN takes its highest value at 4 dimensions. The results are similar for the UNI dataset, as shown in Fig. 5b.

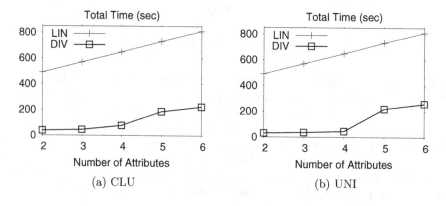

Fig. 5. Effect of $|\mathcal{A}|$

6   Conclusions

The diversification problem is to retrieve a set of objects such that their relevance, measured by distance, to a given query and their diversity, measured by pairwise distance, is maximized. Since it is a computationally hard problem, greedy approaches are typically used. This work introduces the highest diversity gain problem, which is integral in any greedy solution of the diversification problem. We show that for many diversification problems it is possible to define a novelty function that assigns score to objects, so that the most novel object optimally solves the highest diversity gain problem. Based on the study of the novelty function, we proposes an index-based algorithm that is I/O optimal. Experiments have shown that our approach is at least an order of magnitude faster than a recent greedy diversification method, and a simple linear scan.

References

1. Agrawal, R., Gollapudi, S., Halverson, A., Ieong, S.: Diversifying search results. In: WSDM, pp. 5–14 (2009)
2. Angel, A., Koudas, N.: Efficient diversity-aware search. In: SIGMOD, pp. 781–792 (2011)
3. Carbonell, J.G., Goldstein, J.: The use of MMR, diversity-based reranking for reordering documents and producing summaries. In: SIGIR, pp. 335–336 (1998)
4. Demidova, E., Fankhauser, P., Zhou, X., Nejdl, W.: DivQ: diversification for keyword search over structured databases. In: SIGIR, pp. 331–338 (2010)
5. Dou, Z., Hu, S., Chen, K., Song, R., Wen, J.R.: Multi-dimensional search result diversification. In: WSDM, pp. 475–484 (2011)
6. Drosou, M., Pitoura, E.: Search result diversification. SIGMOD Rec. **39**(1), 41–47 (2010)
7. Fagin, R., Lotem, A., Naor, M.: Optimal aggregation algorithms for middleware. In: PODS (2001)
8. Fraternali, P., Martinenghi, D., Tagliasacchi, M.: Top-k bounded diversification. In: SIGMOD, pp. 421–432 (2012)
9. Golenberg, K., Kimelfeld, B., Sagiv, Y.: Keyword proximity search in complex data graphs. In: SIGMOD, pp. 927–940 (2008)
10. Gollapudi, S., Sharma, A.: An axiomatic approach for result diversification. In: WWW, pp. 381–390 (2009)
11. Hassin, R., Rubinstein, S., Tamir, A.: Approximation algorithms for maximum dispersion. Oper. Res. Lett. **21**(3), 133–137 (1997)
12. Ilyas, I.F., Beskales, G., Soliman, M.A.: A survey of top- k query processing techniques in relational database systems. ACM Comput. Surv. **40**(4), 11:1–11:58 (2008)
13. Jain, A., Sarda, P., Haritsa, J.R.: Providing diversity in k-nearest neighbor query results. In: Dai, H., Srikant, R., Zhang, C. (eds.) PAKDD 2004. LNCS (LNAI), vol. 3056, pp. 404–413. Springer, Heidelberg (2004)
14. van Kreveld, M.J., Reinbacher, I., Arampatzis, A., van Zwol, R.: Multi-dimensional scattered ranking methods for geographic information retrieval. GeoInformatica **9**(1), 61–84 (2005)
15. Mei, Q., Guo, J., Radev, D.R.: DivRank: the interplay of prestige and diversity in information networks. In: KDD, pp. 1009–1018 (2010)
16. Qin, L., Yu, J.X., Chang, L.: Diversifying top-k results. VLDB **5**(11), 1124–1135 (2012)
17. Ravi, S., Rosenkrantz, D., Tayi, G.: Heuristic and special case algorithms for dispersion problems. Oper. Res. **42**(2), 299–310 (1994)

18. Sacharidis, D., Deligiannakis, A.: Spatial cohesion queries. In: SIGSPATIAL (2015)
19. Vee, E., Srivastava, U., Shanmugasundaram, J., Bhat, P., Amer-Yahia, S.: Efficient computation of diverse query results. In: ICDE, pp. 228–236 (2008)
20. Vieira, M.R., Razente, H.L., Barioni, M.C.N., Hadjieleftheriou, M., Srivastava, D., Traina Jr., C., Tsotras, V.J.: On query result diversification. In: ICDE, pp. 1163–1174 (2011)
21. Yu, C., Lakshmanan, L.V.S., Amer-Yahia, S.: It takes variety to make a world: diversification in recommender systems. In: EDBT, pp. 368–378 (2009)

Dualization on Partially Ordered Sets: Preliminary Results

Lhouari Nourine[1] and Jean Marc Petit[2(✉)]

[1] Clermont-Université, Université Blaise Pascal, LIMOS, CNRS,
Aubière, France
[2] Université de Lyon, CNRS, LIRIS, INSA, Lyon, France
`jmpetit@liris.cnrs.fr`

Abstract. The dualization problem on arbitrary posets is a crucial step in many applications in logics, databases, artificial intelligence and pattern mining.

The objective of this paper is to study *reductions* of the dualization problem on arbitrary posets to the dualization problem on boolean lattices, for which output quasi-polynomial time algorithms exist. We introduce *convex embedding* and *poset reflection* as key notions to characterize such reductions. As a consequence, we identify posets, which are not boolean lattices, for which the dualization problem remains quasi-polynomial and propose a classification of posets with respect to dualization.

As far as we know, this is the first contribution to explicit non-trivial reductions for studying the hardness of dualization problems on arbitrary posets.

1 Introduction

The dualization problem in arbitrary finite[1] partially ordered sets (poset for short), is a crucial step in many applications in logics, databases, artificial intelligence and pattern mining and has been intensively studied for years [1–3]. The dualization problem can be very difficult and the decision problem associated to dualization is still open, even for lattices. Only a few results exist, mainly dualization is quasi-polynomial whenever $(P, \leq)$ is isomorphic to a powerset ordered under set inclusion (or boolean lattice) [2], which corresponds to the enumeration of minimal transversal of hypergraph.

The dualization problem on hypergraphs has been studied by many researchers, among which we quote [1,2] while only a few results exist on dualization on other posets [4]. Recently Kante *et al.* [5] have shown that the enumeration of minimal transversal of an hypergraph is *equivalent* to the enumeration of minimal dominating sets of a cobipartite graph. Interestingly, this result brings the dualization problem to the large graph theory community.

---

[1] It also works for infinite partially ordered sets that are well ordered, i.e. all antichains are finite.

© Springer International Publishing Switzerland 2016
D. Kotzinos et al. (Eds.): ISIP 2014, CCIS 497, pp. 23–34, 2016.
DOI: 10.1007/978-3-319-38901-1_2

Some theoretical frameworks for pattern mining have studied dualization, for instance [6–8]. In [8], we introduced the idea of weak representations as sets for pattern mining problems and showed how the frequent rigid sequences mining problem benefits from such representation. The embryo of a reduction for the dualization problem on arbitrary posets was present but was clearly implicit in [8].

To measure the complexity of enumeration algorithms, we always refer to the complexity in the size of the input and the size of the output, see [9] for details.

The objective of this paper is to study *reductions* of the dualization problem on arbitrary posets to the dualization problem on boolean lattices. On posets, the dualization problem can be stated as follows:

DualizeOnPoset
Input: A representation of a poset $(P, \leq)$, B^+ an antichain of P.
Output: B^- such that (B^+, B^-) are dual sets[2] in P.

Let us consider the particular instance of this problem:

DualizeOnSet
Input: A finite set E, B^+ an antichain of $\mathcal{P}(E)$ (the powerset of E).
Output: B^- such that (B^+, B^-) are dual sets in $\mathcal{P}(E)$.

As already mentioned, the complexity of **DualizeOnSet** is known to be quasi-polynomial while the complexity of **DualizeOnPoset** is still open in most posets (for example, lattice) [4]. In this setting, we are interested in studying the *reduction* from **DualizeOnPoset** to **DualizeOnSet**, i.e. under which conditions **DualizeOnSet** is at least as hard as **DualizeOnPoset**. Notice that reductions for the hardness of enumeration problems are not well established as for decision problems. In this paper, we consider only polynomial time reduction as explained in Fig. 1 which is inspired from classical polynomial reduction of decision problems.

Contribution on Dualization: We introduce *convex embedding* and *poset reflection* as key notions to characterize such reductions. As a consequence, we identify posets, which are not boolean lattices, for which the dualization problem remains quasi-polynomial and propose a classification of posets with respect to dualization.

2   Preliminaries

We briefly recall definitions on partial orders, embeddings and borders [8,10].

A partial order is a binary relation $\leq$ over a set P which is reflexive, anti-symmetric, and transitive. Let x, y be elements of P, if $x \leq y$ or $y \leq x$, then x and y are comparable, otherwise they are incomparable. A partial order under which every pair of elements is comparable is called a *chain*. A subset of a poset in which no two distinct elements are comparable is called an *antichain*. We say that y covers x if whenever $x \leq z \leq y$ then $z = x$ or $y = z$; we denote by $\prec$ the covering relation. For $S \subseteq P$, $\downarrow S$ (resp. $\uparrow S$) is the downward (resp. upward)

---

[2] Dual sets are also known as blocker and anti-blocker or positive and negative borders.

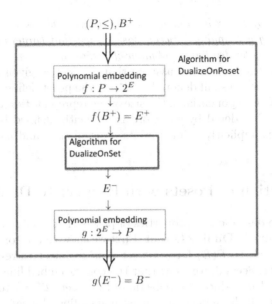

$(P, \leq), B^+$

Polynomial embedding
$f : P \to 2^E$

Algorithm for
DualizeOnPoset

$f(B^+) = E^+$

**Algorithm for
DualizeOnSet**

E^-

Polynomial embedding
$g : 2^E \to P$

$g(E^-) = B^-$

Fig. 1. Reduction from DualizeOnPoset to DualizeOnSet

closed set of S under the relation $\leq$ (i.e. $\downarrow S$ is an ideal and $\uparrow S$ a filter of $(P, \leq)$).
In case of ambiguity, $\downarrow S$ (resp. $\uparrow S$) will be denoted by $\downarrow^{\leq} S$ (resp. $\uparrow^{\leq} S$). A
subset $S \subseteq P$ is *convex* in P if for all $x, y, z \in P$, $x, y \in S$ and $x \leq z \leq y$ implies
$z \in S$. We denote by $Max_{\leq}(S)$ (resp. $Min_{\leq}(S)$) denotes the maximal (resp.
minimal) elements of S with respect to $\leq$. When $\leq$ is clear from context, $(P, \leq)$
(resp. $Max_{\leq}(S)$ and $Min_{\leq}(S)$) will be denoted by P (resp. $Max(S)$, $Min(S)$).

Let $(P, \leq_P)$ and $(Q, \leq_Q)$ be posets and $f : P \to Q$ a mapping (total function).
f is an *embedding* if for all $x, y \in P$, $x \leq_P y$ iff $f(x) \leq_Q f(y)$. The mapping
f is an *isomorphism* if f is a bijective embedding. In this case P and Q are
said to be *isomorphic*. f is a *convex embedding* if f is an *embedding* and $f(P)$
is convex in $(Q, \leq_Q)$. Whenever f is injective but not surjective, there exists
another mapping $g : f(P) \to P$ such that $g \circ f = Id$, the identity function. A
reflection of a poset $(P, \leq)$ is a poset $(P, \leq')$ on the same ground set P such that
for all $x, y \in P$, $x \leq' y \Rightarrow x \leq y$.

Two antichains $(\mathcal{B}^+, \mathcal{B}^-)$ of P are said to be *dual* if $\downarrow \mathcal{B}^+ \cup \uparrow \mathcal{B}^- = P$ and
$\downarrow \mathcal{B}^+ \cap \uparrow \mathcal{B}^- = \emptyset$. The relationship between these dual sets is known as the
dualization, i.e. given $\mathcal{B}^+$, compute $\mathcal{B}^-$ (or inversely). In the sequel, $(\mathcal{B}^+, \mathcal{B}^-)$
will be referred to as a "border".

Let $f : P \to Q$ be a mapping and $(\mathcal{B}^+, \mathcal{B}^-)$ a border in P. The border
$(\mathcal{E}^+, \mathcal{E}^-)$ in Q is an *extension* of $(\mathcal{B}^+, \mathcal{B}^-)$ with respect to f, if $f(\mathcal{B}^+) \subseteq \mathcal{E}^+$ and
$f(\mathcal{B}^-) \subseteq \mathcal{E}^-$. The extension $(\mathcal{E}^+, \mathcal{E}^-)$ is said to be a *polynomial extension* of
$(\mathcal{B}^+, \mathcal{B}^-)$ if $|\mathcal{E}^+| + |\mathcal{E}^-|$ is polynomial in $|\mathcal{B}^+| + |\mathcal{B}^-|$.

The intuition of the reduction of enumeration problems used in this paper is based on finding a mapping between posets such that borders are polynomial preserved, i.e. every border has a polynomial extension.

In the rest of this paper, we assume that a poset is given by an implicit representation $\mathcal{L}$ and we shall denote by $(\mathcal{L}^*, \leq)$ the poset defined by $\mathcal{L}$. Clearly, the size of $\mathcal{L}^*$ may be exponential in the size of the representation $\mathcal{L}$. For instance, the free monoid Σ^* ordered by sub word is implicitly defined by the alphabet Σ, and a lattice is implicitly defined by its poset of (join and meet) irreducible elements [11].

3   Classification of Posets with Respect to Dualization

In this section we describe two properties of posets that lead us to have polynomial time reductions to **DualizeOnSet**. First we show that a convex embedding from a poset $(\mathcal{L}^*, \preceq)$ to $\mathcal{P}(E)$ for some set E is sufficient to re-use algorithms of **DualizeOnSet**. Second, we show that the convex embedding is not a necessary condition and introduce the reflection of a poset $(\mathcal{L}^*, \preceq)$ to obtain a new poset $(\mathcal{L}^*, \preceq')$ in which there is a convex embedding. Indeed, a reflection of a poset $(\mathcal{L}^*, \preceq)$ corresponds to an embedding which preserves incomparabilities (or antichains), even if some comparabilities could be lost. The previous two embeddings introduce extra-elements to the dualization. Whenever these extra-elements are bounded by a polynomial, the dualization can be polynomial reduced to **DualizeOnSet**. To do so, we ask the following questions:

Given a poset of patterns $(\mathcal{L}^*, \preceq)$,

- *Does there exist a convex embedding of $(\mathcal{L}^*, \preceq)$ into $(\mathcal{P}(E), \subseteq)$ for some finite set E? If not,*
- *Does there exist a reflection $(\mathcal{L}^*, \preceq')$ of $(\mathcal{L}^*, \preceq)$ such that there exists a convex embedding of $(\mathcal{L}^*, \preceq')$ into $(\mathcal{P}(E), \subseteq)$ for some finite set E?*

These two questions and their associated computational costs allow to come up with new classes of posets with respect to dualization. Figure 2 gives an illustration with a diagram where posets and borders are placed side by side.

3.1   Convex Embedding

First, let us recall that any poset has an embedding into a boolean lattice.

Proposition 1 [10]. *For any poset $(\mathcal{L}^*, \preceq)$, there exists an embedding from $(\mathcal{L}^*, \preceq)$ to $(\mathcal{P}(E), \subseteq)$, for some finite set E.*

It follows that any poset has a set representation but obviously the dualization on $(\mathcal{L}^*, \preceq)$ may be much more complex than the dualization on $(\mathcal{P}(E), \subseteq)$ [8]. We define the $\mathcal{RAS}$ class as follows:

Definition 1. $(\mathcal{L}^*, \preceq) \in \mathcal{RAS}$ *iff $(\mathcal{L}^*, \preceq)$ and $(\mathcal{P}(E), \subseteq)$ are isomorphic, for some finite set E.*

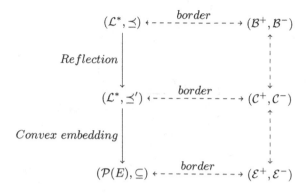

Fig. 2. Reflection and convex embedding

This class of posets gathers together many patterns such as frequent itemsets (FIM) [12], functional dependencies (FD) [13], inclusion dependencies (IND) [14]. This class is known as the *representation as sets* class of pattern mining problems defined in [6].

Nevertheless, requirements to be in $\mathcal{RAS}$ are restrictive, since the poset must be isomorphic to a boolean lattice, and then its size has to be equal to 2^n where $n = |E|$. Now we will relax the bijective constraint of $\mathcal{RAS}$ but we keep the convexity property on the set representation. Hence, we extend $\mathcal{RAS}$ to a new class, called $\mathcal{XRAS}$, for *conveX* $\mathcal{RAS}$.

Definition 2. $(\mathcal{L}^*, \preceq) \in \mathcal{XRAS}$ iff there exists a convex embedding from $(\mathcal{L}^*, \preceq)$ to $(\mathcal{P}(E), \subseteq)$, for some finite set E.

The idea is still to require an isomorphism but just between the poset of patterns and some subset of $\mathcal{P}(E)$, instead of the entire set $\mathcal{P}(E)$ (see Fig. 3). Note also that f is injective since f is an embedding. The following proposition points out a simple yet important characterization of $\mathcal{XRAS}$ problems.

Proposition 2. $(\mathcal{L}^*, \preceq) \in \mathcal{XRAS}$ iff $(\mathcal{L}^*, \preceq)$ is isomorphic to $(\mathcal{P}(E) \backslash (\downarrow B_0^+ \cup \uparrow B_0^-), \subseteq)$ for some antichains $B_0^+ \subseteq \mathcal{P}(E)$ and $B_0^- \subseteq \mathcal{P}(E)$.

Proof. Let f be a convex embedding from $(\mathcal{L}^*, \preceq)$ to $(\mathcal{P}(E), \subseteq)$ and $\mathcal{F} = f(\mathcal{L}^*)$. Let us consider $\mathcal{F}^+ = Min(\mathcal{F})$ and $\mathcal{F}^- = Max(\mathcal{F})$ two antichains of $\mathcal{F}$. Moreover, let $B_0^+ = Max(\{X \in \mathcal{P}(E) | X \subset Y, Y \in F^+\})$ and $B_0^- = Min(\mathcal{P}(E) \backslash (\mathcal{F} \cup \downarrow B_0^+))$. Let $X \in \mathcal{P}(E)$. Then either $X \in \downarrow B_0^+$, or $X \in \uparrow B_0^-$ or $X \in \mathcal{P}(E) \backslash (\downarrow B_0^+ \cup \uparrow B_0^-)$. In the latter case, there exists $Y_1 \in F^+, Y_2 \in F^-$ such that $Y_1 \subseteq X \subseteq Y_2$. Since $\mathcal{F}$ is convex, $X \in \mathcal{F}$ and the result follows.

The other direction holds since $\mathcal{P}(E) \backslash (\downarrow B_0^+ \cup \uparrow B_0^-)$ is a convex set of $\mathcal{P}(E)$.   □

Figure 3 gives an illustration of the Proposition 2.

Note that the sets B_0^+ and B_0^- can be exponential in the size of E. The next definition introduces *efficient* problems of $\mathcal{XRAS}$, called $\mathcal{EXRAS}$.

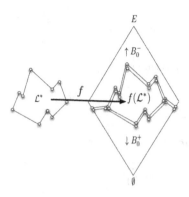

Fig. 3. The class $\mathcal{XRAS}$

Definition 3. $(\mathcal{L}^*, \preceq) \in \mathcal{EXRAS}$ *if* $(\mathcal{L}^*, \preceq) \in \mathcal{XRAS}$ *and* $|B_0^+ \cup B_0^-|$ *is polynomial in* $|E|$.

The following proposition points out that a polynomial extension of any border of $(\mathcal{L}^*, \preceq)$ exists if $(\mathcal{L}^*, \preceq) \in \mathcal{EXRAS}$.

Proposition 3. *Let* $(\mathcal{L}^*, \preceq) \in \mathcal{EXRAS}$ *and* $f : \mathcal{L}^* \to \mathcal{P}(E)$ *a convex embedding, for some finite set* E.
Then for any border $(\mathcal{B}^+, \mathcal{B}^-)$ *of* $(\mathcal{L}^*, \preceq)$, $(Max(B_0^+ \cup f(\mathcal{B}^+)), Min(B_0^- \cup f(\mathcal{B}^-)))$ *is a polynomial extension of* $(\mathcal{B}^+, \mathcal{B}^-)$ *in* $(\mathcal{P}(E), \subseteq)$.

Proof. It suffices to notice that $(\mathcal{B}^+, \mathcal{B}^-)$ is a border of $(\mathcal{L}^*, \preceq)$ iff $(f(\mathcal{B}^+), f(\mathcal{B}^-))$ is a border of $(\mathcal{P}(E) \backslash (\downarrow B_0^+ \cup \uparrow B_0^-), \subseteq)$ since $(\mathcal{L}^*, \preceq)$ is isomorphic to $(\mathcal{P}(E) \backslash (\downarrow B_0^+ \cup \uparrow B_0^-), \subseteq)$. □

3.2 Polynomial Reflection of Posets

We now consider posets that are not in $\mathcal{XRAS}$. Our idea is to transform the initial poset to a new poset over the same ground set, in order to get a convex embedding. As a consequence, two natural question arise:

(1) For a given poset $(\mathcal{L}^*, \preceq)$, does there exist a "polynomial reflection" $(\mathcal{L}^*, \preceq')$ such that $(\mathcal{L}^*, \preceq')$ belongs to $\mathcal{EXRAS}$?
(2) How to quantify the "lost comparabilities" induced by a reflection?

In the sequel, we study poset reflection to give answers to the previous questions. Since the reflection of a poset induces the lost of some comparabilities in the original poset, we have to recover them efficiently.

Before that, we consider different examples of posets over sequences.

Examples with Different Posets of Sequences. Let us consider sequences with or without wildcard (denoted $\star$), see e.g. [15].

Let Σ be an alphabet. A sequence is an element of Σ^* and a rigid sequence an element of $(\Sigma \cup \{\star\})^*$ of the form $P = P[1] \cdots P[m]$ such that $P[1] \neq \star$ and $P[m] \neq \star$. Let Σ_R^* be the set of rigid sequences and Σ^* the set of sequences. We denote by Σ^n the set of all sequences in Σ^* of size at most n.

Different partial orders over Σ_R^* and Σ^* exist. Let us first consider sub-word (resp. factor and prefix) posets over Σ^*, denoted $(\Sigma^*, \leq_s)$ (resp. $(\Sigma^*, \leq_f)$ and $(\Sigma^*, \leq_p)$). Let $P[1..m], Q[1..n] \in \Sigma^*$. We have:

- $P \leq_s Q$ if there exists integers $i_1 < \ldots < i_m$ in $[1..n]$ such that $P[j] = Q[i_j]$ for all $j \in [1..m]$.
- $P \leq_f Q$ if $P \leq_s Q$ and $i_j = i_{j+1} - 1$ for all $j \in [1..m-1]$
- $P \leq_p Q$ if $P \leq_f Q$ and $i_m = m$.

These different posets are illustrated in Fig. 4 on a simple example.

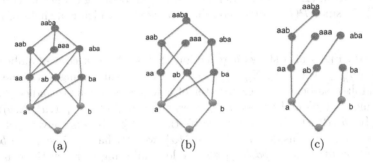

Fig. 4. (a) The sub word poset induced by the word w=aaba on $\Sigma = \{a, b\}$; (b) the factor poset which is a reflection of (a); and (c) the prefix poset which is a reflection of posets (b) and (a).

In Fig. 4, let us consider the set $\{aa, ab\}$ for the different posets. Its dual set is equal to $\{ba, aab, aaa\}$ for (a) and (b) and $\{b, aab, aaa, aba\}$ for (c).

Second, we consider two posets for rigid sequences, one similar to the factor poset and another one to the prefix poset, denoted $(\Sigma_R^*, \sqsubseteq)$ and $(\Sigma_R^*, \sqsubseteq_1)$. Let $P[1..m], Q[1..n] \in \Sigma_R^*$. We have:

- $P \sqsubseteq Q$ if there exists $p \in [1..n]$ such that for every $i \in [1..m]$, either $P[i] = Q[p + i - 1]$ or $P[i] = \star$
- $P \sqsubseteq_1 Q$ if for every $i \in [1..m]$, either $P[i] = Q[i]$ or $P[i] = \star$

These two posets are illustrated in Fig. 5, where the poset (b) suggests the existence of hidden hypercubes in the poset (a).

Now, we claim that the posets $(\Sigma^*, \leq_s)$, $(\Sigma^*, \leq_f)$, $(\Sigma^*, \leq_p)$ and $(\Sigma_R^*, \sqsubseteq)$ do not have any convex embedding. Consider again the example given in Fig. 4 and the two following sets: $A = \{a, b, ab, ba\}$ and $A' = \{a, aa, aaa\}$.

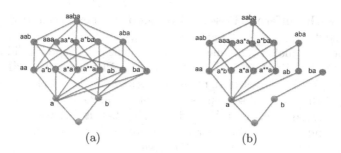

Fig. 5. (a) The factor poset of rigid sequences induced by the word w=aaba on $\Sigma = \{a, b\}$; (b) the prefix poset of rigid sequences which is a reflection of posets (a).

- A is convex in $(\Sigma^*, \leq_s)$ (Fig. 4(a)) but its image by any embedding cannot be convex in $(\mathcal{P}(E), \subseteq)$ since $(\mathcal{P}(E), \subseteq)$ is a lattice. The same reasoning applies for $(\Sigma^*, \leq_f)$ and $(\Sigma_R^*, \sqsubseteq)$.
- A' is convex in $(\Sigma^*, \leq_p)$ but its image by any embedding cannot be convex in $(\mathcal{P}(E), \subseteq)$ since $\mathcal{P}(E)$ cannot contain a convex set which is a chain of length 3.

However, Fig. 5 also shows a reflection that leads to a convex embedding. Consider $(\Sigma_R^n, \sqsubseteq_1)$. Let $f : \Sigma_R^n \setminus \{\epsilon\} \to \mathcal{P}(E)$ be an embedding, for some finite set E [8,15]: f associates to each letter of a sequence a couple (indice, letter). For instance, let ab and ba be two patterns. Then $f(ab) = \{(1, a), (2, b)\}$ and $f(ba) = \{(1, b), (2, a)\}$. It is easy to verify that $f(\Sigma_R^n \setminus \{\epsilon\})$ is convex in $(\mathcal{P}(E), \subseteq)$ [8]. Let us again consider $A = \{a, b, ab, ba\}$: we only have $a \sqsubseteq_1 ab, b \sqsubseteq_1 ba$, i.e. two comparabilities ($a \not\sqsubseteq_1 ba, b \not\sqsubseteq_1 ab$) are lost, allowing to reach the convexity constraint.

These examples point out that we have to study poset reflection to be able to obtain some convex embedding.

3.3 Reaching Convexity by Poset Reflection

As shown in previous examples involving sequences, whenever possible, we have now to quantify the lost comparabilities induced by a poset reflection.

For a given element of a poset, we define its successors and its predecessors induced by a poset reflection.

Definition 4. *Let* $(P, \leq')$ *a reflection of a poset* $(P, \leq)$ *and* $x \in P$. *The lost predecessors of* x *in the reflection of* $(P, \leq)$ *to* $(P, \leq')$, *denoted by* LostPred(x), *are defined by:*
LostPred$(x) = Max_{\leq'}\{y \in P | y \leq x, y \not\leq' x\}$. *Similarly, the lost successors are defined by:* LostSucc$(x) = Min_{\leq'}\{y \in P | x \leq y, x \not\leq' y\}$.

By extension, we note LostPred$(X) = \bigcup_{x \in X}$ LostPred(x) *(resp.* LostSucc $(X))$ *for* $X \subseteq P$.

Example 1. Let us consider the reflection $(\Sigma_R^n, \sqsubseteq_1)$ of $(\Sigma_R^n, \sqsubseteq)$ [8]. Let $S \in \Sigma_R^n$. We have $\texttt{LostPred}(S) = \{S[i..|S|] \mid 1 \le i \le |S|, S[i] \ne \star\}$ and $\texttt{LostSucc}(S) = \{x \underbrace{\star \ldots \star}_{i} S \mid 0 \le i \le n - |S| - 1, x \in \Sigma\}$.

For instance with $n = 5$, $\texttt{LostPred}(a \star ba) = \{a \star ba, ba, a\}$ and $\texttt{LostSucc}(ba) = \{aba, bba, a \star ba, b \star ba, a \star \star ba, b \star \star ba\}$.

As shown in the following lemma, we can recover the initial poset from any reduced poset with $\texttt{LostPred}$ and $\texttt{LostSucc}$.

Lemma 1. *Let $x \in P$ and $(P, \le')$ a reflection of $(P, \le)$. Then:*

1. $\downarrow^{\le} x = \downarrow^{\le'} \texttt{LostPred}(x)$ *and*
2. $\uparrow^{\le} x = \uparrow^{\le'} \texttt{LostSucc}(x)$.

Proof. (1) Let $y \in \downarrow^{\le} x$. We have either $y \le' x$ or $y \not\le' x$. If $y \le' x$, then $y \in \downarrow^{\le'} \texttt{LostPred}(x)$ since $x \in \texttt{LostPred}(x)$. If $y \not\le' x$, then there exists $z \in P$ such that $y \le' z, z \in \texttt{LostPred}(x)$, i.e. $y \in \downarrow^{\le'} \texttt{LostPred}(x)$. The same reasoning applies for (2). □

Some remarks have to be made: First, for any poset, there always exists a reflection that has a convex embedding into a boolean lattice. It suffices to take a reflection which is an antichain, i.e. that deletes all comparabilities. In this case, the number of lost comparabilities can be exponential in the size of the description of the poset. Second, we would like to be able to recover lost comparabilities in polynomial time. This is formalized with the notion of *poly-reflection* as follows.

Definition 5. $(\mathcal{L}^*, \preceq')$ *is a poly-reflection of* $(\mathcal{L}^*, \preceq)$ *if* $(\mathcal{L}^*, \preceq')$ *is a reflection of* $(\mathcal{L}^*, \preceq)$ *and for all $x \in \mathcal{L}^*$, $\texttt{LostPred}(x)$ and $\texttt{LostSucc}(x)$ are computable in polynomial time in the size of the description $\mathcal{L}$.*

Example 2. Continuing the previous example, for all $S \in \Sigma_R^n$, $\texttt{LostPred}(S)$ is polynomial in n and for all $s \sqsubseteq S$, there exists $s' \in \texttt{LostPred}(S)$ such that $s \sqsubseteq_1 s'$. Therefore, $(\Sigma_R^n, \sqsubseteq_1)$ is a poly-reflection of $(\Sigma_R^n, \sqsubseteq)$.

Now we show the relationship between borders in a poset and its reflection. For a given border on the initial poset, we define its extension in the reduced poset to take into account lost comparabilities.

Definition 6. *Let* $(\mathcal{L}^*, \preceq')$ *be a poly-reflection of* $(\mathcal{L}^*, \preceq)$ *and* $(\mathcal{B}^+, \mathcal{B}^-)$ *a border of* $(\mathcal{L}^*, \preceq)$. *The extension of* $(\mathcal{B}^+, \mathcal{B}^-)$ *in* $(\mathcal{L}^*, \preceq')$, *denoted by* $(\mathbf{ext}(\mathcal{B}^+), \mathbf{ext}(\mathcal{B}^-))$, *is defined by:*
$$\mathbf{ext}(\mathcal{B}^+) = Max_{\le'}\{\texttt{LostPred}(x) \mid x \in \mathcal{B}^+\}$$
$$\mathbf{ext}(\mathcal{B}^-) = Min_{\le'}\{\texttt{LostSucc}(x) \mid x \in \mathcal{B}^-\}.$$

The "preservation" of borders can now be formally stated.

Proposition 4. *Let* $(\mathcal{L}^*, \preceq')$ *be a poly-reflection of* $(\mathcal{L}^*, \preceq)$ *and* $(\mathcal{B}^+, \mathcal{B}^-)$ *a border of* $(\mathcal{L}^*, \preceq)$. *Then* $(\mathbf{ext}(\mathcal{B}^+), \mathbf{ext}(\mathcal{B}^-))$ *is a polynomial extension of* $(\mathcal{B}^+, \mathcal{B}^-)$.

Proof. We have to show:

1. $(\mathbf{ext}(\mathcal{B}^+), \mathbf{ext}(\mathcal{B}^-))$ is a border of $(\mathcal{L}^*, \preceq')$ with $\mathcal{B}^+ \subseteq \mathbf{ext}(\mathcal{B}^+)$ and $\mathcal{B}^- \subseteq \mathbf{ext}(\mathcal{B}^-)$,
2. $|\mathbf{ext}(\mathcal{B}^+)| + |\mathbf{ext}(\mathcal{B}^-)|$ is polynomial in $|\mathcal{B}^+| + |\mathcal{B}^-|$.

(1) Any reflection preserves all incomparabilities and $x \in \mathtt{LostPred}(x)$ (resp $x \in \mathtt{LostSucc}(x)$) for all $x \in \mathcal{L}^*$. Then $\mathcal{B}^+ \subseteq \mathbf{ext}(\mathcal{B}^+)$ and $\mathcal{B}^- \subseteq \mathbf{ext}(\mathcal{B}^-)$. By definition, $\mathbf{ext}(\mathcal{B}^+)$ and $\mathbf{ext}(\mathcal{B}^-)$ are antichains in $(\mathcal{L}^*, \preceq')$. By Lemma 1, the result follows.

(2) $|\mathbf{ext}(\mathcal{B}^+)| + |\mathbf{ext}(\mathcal{B}^-)|$ is polynomial in $|\mathcal{B}^+| + |\mathcal{B}^-|$ since $(\mathcal{L}^*, \preceq')$ is a poly-reflection of $(\mathcal{L}^*, \preceq)$ since computing $\mathtt{LostPred}(x)$ and $\mathtt{LostSucc}(x)$ can be done in polynomial time in the size of the description of $\mathcal{L}$. ☐

The notion of poly-reflection allows to define the last class of posets, called $\mathcal{EWRAS}$, meaning *Efficient weak representation as sets*. $\mathcal{EWRAS}$ is the more general class ensuring the existence of quasi-polynomial algorithms. It combines both poly-reflection of posets and $\mathcal{EXRAS}$.

Definition 7. $(\mathcal{L}^*, \preceq) \in \mathcal{EWRAS}$ *iff there exists a poly-reflection $(\mathcal{L}^*, \preceq')$ of $(\mathcal{L}^*, \preceq)$ such that $(\mathcal{L}^*, \preceq') \in \mathcal{EXRAS}$.*

Then, this definition means that if some comparabilities can be forgotten – up to a polynomial cost to recover them – to get a new poset satisfying the condition of $\mathcal{EXRAS}$, then the dualization problem on the initial poset can be reduced to **DualizationOnSet**.

Example 3. Continuing previous examples, we have $(\Sigma_R^*, \sqsubseteq_1)$ is a poly-reflection of $(\Sigma_R^*, \sqsubseteq)$ and $(\Sigma_R^*, \sqsubseteq_1)$ belongs to $\mathcal{EXRAS}$. Then, $(\Sigma_R^*, \sqsubseteq)$ belongs to $\mathcal{EWRAS}$.

The main result concerning the $\mathcal{EWRAS}$ class is now given:

Theorem 1. *Let $(\mathcal{L}^*, \preceq) \in \mathcal{EWRAS}$. Assume that $(\mathcal{L}^*, \preceq')$ is a poly-reflection of $(\mathcal{L}^*, \preceq)$ such that $(\mathcal{L}^*, \preceq')$ belongs to $\mathcal{EXRAS}$, i.e. $(\mathcal{L}^*, \preceq')$ isomorphic to $\mathcal{P}(E) \setminus (B_0^+ \cup B_0^-)$. Then, for any border $(\mathcal{B}^+, \mathcal{B}^-)$ of $(\mathcal{L}^*, \preceq)$:*

- $(B_0^+ \cup f(\mathbf{ext}(\mathcal{B}^+)), B_0^- \cup f(\mathbf{ext}(\mathcal{B}^-)))$ *is a border in $(\mathcal{P}(E), \subseteq)$,*
- $(B_0^+ \cup f(\mathbf{ext}(\mathcal{B}^+)), B_0^- \cup f(\mathbf{ext}(\mathcal{B}^-)))$ *is a polynomial extension of $(\mathcal{B}^+, \mathcal{B}^-)$,*

The following corollary gives the relationship between all the classes introduced so far.

Corollary 1. *Let $(\mathcal{L}^*, \preceq')$ be a poly-reflection of $(\mathcal{L}^*, \preceq)$ such that $(\mathcal{L}^*, \preceq')$ belongs to $\mathcal{XRAS}$, i.e. $(\mathcal{L}^*, \preceq')$ isomorphic to $\mathcal{P}(E) \setminus (B_0^+ \cup B_0^-)$. We have:*

1. $(\mathcal{L}^*, \preceq) \in \mathcal{RAS}$ *if $(\mathcal{L}^*, \preceq) = (\mathcal{L}^*, \preceq')$ and $B_0^+ = B_0^- = \emptyset$.*
2. $(\mathcal{L}^*, \preceq) \in \mathcal{XRAS}$ *if $(\mathcal{L}^*, \preceq) = (\mathcal{L}^*, \preceq')$.*
3. $(\mathcal{L}^*, \preceq) \in \mathcal{EXRAS}$ *if $(\mathcal{L}^*, \preceq) = (\mathcal{L}^*, \preceq')$ and the size of $B_0^+ \cup B_0^-$ is polynomial in the size of the description of $(\mathcal{L}^*, \preceq)$.*
4. $(\mathcal{L}^*, \preceq) \in \mathcal{EWRAS}$ *if the size of $B_0^+ \cup B_0^-$ is polynomial in the size of the description of $(\mathcal{L}^*, \preceq)$.*

3.4 DualizeOnSeq is Equivalent to DualizeOnSet

Recall that we consider rigid sequences only. The dualization problem can be stated as follows:

DualizeOnSeq
Input: Σ a totally ordered alphabet with a minimal element $\star$, n a positive integer, B^+ a positive border of Σ_R^n.
output: B^- such that (B^+, B^-) is a border of Σ_R^n.

We have already showed that **DualizeOnSeq** is at least as hard as **DualizeOnSet** in [8]. In the sequel, we point out that **DualizeOnSet** is at least as hard as **DualizeOnSeq**, and therefore the two problems are polynomially equivalent. Indeed, we show that **DualizeOnSet** is a particular case of **DualizeOnSeq**.

Let $\Sigma = \{1, 2, ..., n, \star\}$ be an ordered alphabet (i.e. $\star < 1 < 2... < n$ and $S \in \Sigma^n$. The sequence S is said to be an *ordered sequence* if for any $i, j \in [1..n]$ such that $i < j$, $S[i] \neq \star$ and $S[j] \neq \star$ we have $S[j] - S[i] = j - i$. We denote $\Sigma_O^n \subseteq \Sigma^n$ the set of all ordered sequences of size at most n. For example, the sequence $2 \star \star 5$ is an ordered sequence but $2 \star 5$ is not.

The following lemma characterizes ordered sequences.

Lemma 2. *Let $\Sigma = \{1, 2, ..., n, \star\}$ be an ordered alphabet and $S \in \Sigma^n$. Then $S \in \Sigma_O^n$ iff S does not contain a subsequence of the form $i \underbrace{\star ... \star}_{k} j$ with either $i < j$ and $k \neq j - i - 1$, or $i \geq j$ with $k \in [0..n - 2]$.*

Consider the set $B_0^- = \{i *^k j \mid i \geq j, k \in [0..n - 2]\} \cup \{i *^k j \mid i < j, k \in [0..n - 2], k \neq j - i - 1\}$. For example for $\Sigma = \{1, 2, 3, *\}$ we have $B_0^- = \{11, 1 * 1, 22, 2 * 2, 33, 3 * 3, 21, 2 * 1, 31, 3 * 1, 32, 3 * 2\} \cup \{13\}$.

Lemma 3. $\Sigma^n \backslash \uparrow B_0^- = \Sigma_O^n$.

Let $V = \{1, ..., n\}$ be a set. We define the mapping $f : \mathcal{P}(V) \to \Sigma^n$ such that for any $E \in \mathcal{P}(V)$, $f(E) = S$ with $S[i] = i$ if $i \in E$ and $S[i] = \star$ otherwise. Without loss of generality, we delete the symbols $\star$ that are prefix or suffix of $f(E)$. Note that $f(E)[i] = \star$ means that $i \notin E$. For example $f(\{2, 5\}) = 2 \star \star 5$ and $f(\{\})$ is the empty sequence.

Proposition 5. *Let $V = \{1, ..., n\}$ be a set. Then the mapping f is a convex embedding of $\mathcal{P}(V)$ into Σ^n. Moreover $f(\mathcal{P}(V)) = \Sigma_O^n$.*

Proof. Let P, Q be two sequences that are images of two sets $A \subset B \subseteq V$, i.e. $f(A) = P$ and $f(B) = Q$. Clearly $f(A) \sqsubseteq f(B)$.

Now suppose there is a sequence S such that $P \sqsubseteq S \sqsubseteq Q$.

For every $i \neq j \in [1..n]$ we have either $S[i] \neq S[j]$ or $S[i] = S[j] = \star$, by definition of the embedding f. Then the set $C = \{x \in V \mid S[i] = x, i \in [1..n]\}$ is clearly defined. Moreover $f(C) = S$ and $A \subset C \subset B$, since for any $x \in \Sigma$, $x \not\sqsubseteq \star$, but $\star \sqsubseteq x$.

We have $f(\mathcal{P}(V)) = \Sigma_O^n$ by construction. $\square$

Theorem 2. *DualizeOnSeq and DualizeOnSet are polynomially equivalent.*

Proof. We have shown that **DualizeOnSeq** is polynomially reducible to **DualizeOnSet** [8]. In Proposition 5, we have shown the existence of a convex embedding from $\mathcal{P}(V)$ into Σ^n. Moreover we have shown that $B_0^+ = \emptyset$ and according to Lemma 2 the size of B_0^- is bounded by $O(n^3)$. Thus **DualizeOnSet** is polynomially reducible to **DualizeOnSeq**.   □

We have shown that the dualization on rigid sequences with wildcard is equivalent to the dualization on set, i.e. enumerating minimal transversals of a given hypergraph.

References

1. Eiter, T., Gottlob, G.: Identifying the minimal transversals of a hypergraph and related problems. SIAM J. Comput. **24**(6), 1278–1304 (1995)
2. Fredman, M.L., Khachiyan, L.: On the complexity of dualization of monotone disjunctive normal forms. J. Algorithms **21**(3), 618–628 (1996)
3. Eiter, T., Gottlob, G., Makino, K.: New results on monotone dualization and generating hypergraph transversals. SIAM J. Comput. **32**, 514–537 (2003)
4. Elbassioni, K.M.: Algorithms for dualization over products of partially ordered sets. SIAM J. Discrete Math. **23**(1), 487–510 (2009)
5. Kanté, M.M., Limouzy, V., Mary, A., Nourine, L.: On the enumeration of minimal dominating sets and related notions. Revised version submitted (2013)
6. Mannila, H., Toivonen, H.: Levelwise search and borders of theories in knowledge discovery. Data Min. Knowl. Discov. **1**(3), 241–258 (1997)
7. Gunopulos, D., Khardon, R., Mannila, H., Saluja, S., Toivonen, H., Sharm, R.S.: Discovering all most specific sentences. ACM Trans. Database Syst. **28**(2), 140–174 (2003)
8. Nourine, L., Petit, J.M.: Extending set-based dualization: application to pattern mining. In: Press, I. (ed.) ECAI 2012, August 2012
9. Elbassioni, K.: Incremental algorithms for enumerating extremal solutions of monotone systems of submodular inequality and their applications. Ph.D. thesis, Rutgers, The state university of New Jersey (2002)
10. Davey, B.A., Priestley, H.A.: Introduction to Lattices and Order. Cambridge Press, New York (1990)
11. Ganter, B., Wille, R.: Formal Concept Analysis. Springer, Heidelberg (1999)
12. Agrawal, R., Imielinski, T., Swami, A.: Mining associations between sets of items in massive databases. In: ACM SIGMOD 1993, Washington D.C., pp. 207–216 (1993)
13. Mannila, H., Rih, K.J.: Algorithms for inferring functional dependencies from relations. Data Knowl. Eng. **12**(1), 83–99 (1994)
14. De Marchi, F., Petit, J.M.: Zigzag: a new algorithm for mining large inclusion dependencies in databases. In: ICDM 2003, USA, pp. 27–34, November 2003
15. Arimura, H., Uno, T.: Polynomial-delay and polynomial-space algorithms for mining closed sequences, graphs, and pictures in accessible set systems. In: SDM, pp. 1087–1098 (2009)

Continuous Top-k Processing
of Social Network Information Streams: A Vision

Abdulhafiz Alkhouli, Dan Vodislav[✉], and Boris Borzic

ETIS, ENSEA, University of Cergy-Pontoise, CNRS, Cergy, France
dan.vodislav@u-cergy.fr

Abstract. With the huge popularity of social networks, publishing and consuming content through information streams is nowadays at the heart of the new Web. Top-k queries over the streams of interest allow limiting results to relevant content, while continuous processing of such queries is the most effective approach in large scale systems. Current systems fail in combining continuous top-k processing with rich scoring models including social network criteria. We present in this paper our vision on the possible features of a social network of information streams, with a rich scoring model compatible with continuous top-k processing.

Keywords: Information streams · Social networks · Continuous top-k query processing

1 Introduction

The advent of Web 2.0 technologies has deeply changed the way information is published and consumed on the Web. Passive readers have become both active information collectors and producers, while dynamic content generation and consumption has continuously gained importance compared to traditional Web publishing (of Web pages) and exploring (through bookmarks, search engines and hyperlink navigation).

Content publishing takes more and more the form of *information streams* available through various information channels: RSS/Atom feeds from newspapers and media, blogs, discussion forums, social networks, etc. Information streams consist of flows of items, usually short semi-structured text messages, possibly containing links to some Web resources (images, videos, pages, etc.), and continuously published through specific diffusion channels. Users may subscribe to several information channels of interest and continuously receive on it, in real-time, new published content. With the huge popularity of social networks and of other information stream sources, this method of publishing and consuming content is today at the heart of the new Web.

An important dimension in this publish-subscribe (pub/sub) framework is the relationship between publishers of information streams and subscribers. This *social network dimension* varies from no relationship at all in the case of RSS/Atom feeds, to possible interaction with the published messages on blogs

© Springer International Publishing Switzerland 2016
D. Kotzinos et al. (Eds.): ISIP 2014, CCIS 497, pp. 35–48, 2016.
DOI: 10.1007/978-3-319-38901-1_3

(comments) and discussion forums (reply messages), and to explicit relationships between users playing the double role of publishers and subscribers on social networks such as Facebook (symmetric "friendship" relations) or Twitter (asymmetric "following" relations). The social network dimension contributes not only with providing information streams of interest to end users, but also comes with criteria to measure this potential interest.

If this pub/sub approach in content dissemination has many advantages in facilitating the access to continuously delivered, fresh, pertinent information, it also raises some significant challenges. Maybe the most important one is *the huge amount of information* available on today information channels; for a regular user, the number of potentially interesting information streams combined with the flow of messages they deliver, leads to overwhelming amounts of information. Even if channels are organized by thematic criteria to help users choosing information streams of interest, not all the published content is useful or equally useful to them. The first challenge is then to define models for filtering and ranking content, and to provide easy to use subscription languages and tools for managing delivered information.

One way to organize the large amounts of stream messages is to define *a ranking model* based on *the importance of a message relative to a given subscription query*. Measuring this importance by a score allows end users to identify and to focus on the most important messages for them, e.g. those with a score over a given threshold, or the k most important ones (top-k). The ranking model may depend on various context factors, among which we emphasize the following ones:

- *Content* based factors, measuring the adequacy of the message content with the subscription query. Since textual content is characteristic to information streams, content-based subscription queries are usually based on sets of terms of interest, and the importance of a message is evaluated from an information retrieval perspective, as the relevance of the text message to the query, based on popular models such as tf-idf [26] or BM25 [17].
- *User* based factors, measuring the importance of users and of their relationships in the social network, for instance the importance of the message publisher and of the relationship between the subscriber and the publisher. In most cases user-based importance is measured on the social network graph, by evaluating e.g. node centrality and distance between nodes.
- *Interaction* based factors, measuring the importance of messages by the reaction they provoked, expressed through actions of other users on that message. Depending on the social network context, current actions may be likes, comments, forwards, tagging as favorite, etc.
- *Time* based factors, measuring the decrease of importance for a message as time goes by. Two main approaches are used to take into account this dimension: sliding time windows [13], resulting in dropping messages older than a given duration, and time decay functions [28,29], expressing a continuous decrease of importance.

Other context factors, that we do not consider here, may contribute to evaluate the importance of messages, such as geographic location or other information elements specific to the social network and to the pub/sub environment.

The second main challenge in the pub/sub approach for information streams is the design and implementation of *efficient processing models* at a very large scale (millions, up to billions of users and information streams). In the case of ranking models based on scoring functions, where subscription results are limited to the most important messages, the main difficulty comes from the need of continuously (re-)computing the score of every message relative to every subscription query and of subsequently maintaining the lists of subscription results. The complexity of this task depends not only on the number of messages and queries, but also on the form of the scoring function.

Two main categories of processing models have been proposed in this context. *The static approach* is based on periodic snapshot queries over the set of published messages to get the list of important messages for each user. *The continuous approach* handles subscriptions as continuous queries reacting to new messages and to other events, in order to incrementally maintain the important messages. As illustrated by the related work below, if the continuous approach is more efficient, it also has more difficulties to handle complex scoring functions. To the best of our knowledge, the continuous methods proposed so far only explored simple scoring functions, most of the time based on the textual content, eventually combined with time factors. More complex scoring, including social network factors has been proposed, but only handled through a static approach.

This paper considers, in the general context introduced above, the problem of continuously computing top-k messages for each subscription query in a very large information stream pub/sub system, including complex scoring functions corresponding to a social network environment. We describe our vision of this problem in the context of state-of-the-art related work, and propose a general model of social network information streams covering many existing cases, a scoring model in this context including all the importance factors introduced above, and finally a processing architecture for continuous top-k processing in the defined context.

The rest of the paper is organized as follows: next section presents related work, Sect. 3 describes the social network model and the scoring function, then Sect. 4 presents an architecture for continuous top-k processing, before concluding.

2   Related Work

Information Stream Filtering. Several approaches have been proposed to tackle the problem of reducing the amount of information received from streams by filtering their contents. If the first RSS/Atom feed aggregation tools (Google Reader, NetVibes[1], etc.) did not initially consider filtering, the need for controlling the volume and for personalizing the content of received information rapidly led to the introduction of various, complex filtering criteria, such as in Yahoo! Pipes[2].

---

[1] http://www.netvibes.com.

[2] https://pipes.yahoo.com/pipes/.

Boolean filtering has been first proposed for information streams, using filters based on Boolean predicates. Most cases focus on text filtering through Boolean keyword predicates, in a pub/sub context. Such solutions [15,33] come with various index structures for fast detection of the subscription queries concerned by a stream input message, in the context of a large number of subscriptions. In [7], keyword subscriptions are considered in the context of a micro-blogging social network and three index structures are proposed; they use three dimensions (keywords/terms, publishers and followers) to enrich indexing with the structure of the social network.

The drawback of Boolean filtering is that the number of results may be in some cases too big or too small. *Information retrieval (IR) ranking models*, such as tf-idf [26] or Okapi BM25 [17] provide ranking of results through a relevance score computed for each message in the context of a given text query. Relevance scores and ranking allow selecting the best results and adapting their number to the end user needs.

Two main approaches have been proposed for filtering stream messages in an IR ranking context. The first one uses *a predefined threshold* for the relevance score [6, 25,32,34]. However, finding the right threshold in a given context is a difficult task and [36] proposes a method for adaptive detection of this threshold. More recent work [14,21,24,28,29] has adopted the second approach, of *top-k computation*, by considering only the k most relevant results in a continuous processing approach. The additional difficulty in this case, compared to threshold-based ranking, is to continuously maintain a changing list of top-k results.

We mention here also some work on *filtering data (non-textual) streams*, where items are composed of vectors of typed values, numerical in most cases. Boolean filtering is considered in [1,3,10], where various indexes for Boolean data predicates from subscription queries are proposed. Ranking for top-k filtering in this context [8,20] is based on multidimensional indexes for numerical vectors and faces the same problems related to the curse of dimensionality as for multimedia features indexing, which limits the number of dimensions for which these structures are efficient.

In this context, our work addresses top-k filtering for information streams in a social network environment, going beyond text-only messages. The social network parameters and possibly non-textual message components require solutions which combine IR text ranking methods with specific index structures.

Score Model. In ranking models for information streams, the importance of a stream message for a subscription query has been generally considered in the context of text messages and queries, based on IR text relevance models such as tf-idf and BM25. To this query-dependent score model, some approaches have also added a *global, query independent importance of messages*, based on the PageRank score [22] when messages refer web pages, on information novelty [12], on source authority [9,16] or on user attention [30].

The social network context has been considered in the scoring models, in order to improve the relevance of subscription query results by taking into account the relationships between publishers and subscribers. Social network components are included in the score model in several approaches, such as the distance in the social graph [2,35], user actions [18] or spatial information [31].

However, the complexity of these scoring models prevented their use for continuous top-k processing. Either they are only proposed to provide a better relevance estimation in social network environments, or, at best, they come with efficient algorithms for score components computation (e.g. distance in graph) and with static, snapshot-based algorithms for top-k evaluation [31,35]. To the best of our knowledge, the only work on continuous top-k processing for information streams including a social network component in its score model is [29], but this is limited to the simplest component, a global, query independent importance of each message.

In the context of *social tagging networks*, such as Delicious or Flickr, score models with social network components have also been proposed. [19,27] consider score models combining text and social relevance, and provide snapshot-based algorithms for top-k computation.

However, we do not consider tagging networks as producing information streams; even if some analogy may be considered between documents/tags in tagging networks and messages/actions in our information stream networks, there are too many differences between their models to generalize a realistic common social network model.

In this context, our work aims at proposing a rich score model, including social network components, providing a good compromise between expressiveness and complexity for continuous top-k processing of information streams.

Continuous Top-k Processing. The closest work to our approach concerns continuous top-k processing models for information streams. [23] is an early work on probabilistic models for continuous top-k processing with a time sliding window w (top-k/w publish-subscribe), independently on a scoring model. [21] proposes a solution for top-k/w publish-subscribe over text message streams based on classical tf-idf cosine similarity. It uses two inverted text indexes, one for the most recent messages (in the sliding window) and the second one for the subscription queries. Top-k processing is based on the Threshold Algorithm (TA) [11] exploiting the text indexes. However, since messages are indexed, a high arrival rate results here in expensive index updates.

[14] also tackles top-k/w publish-subscribe on text information streams and proposes the COL-Filter algorithm and an improved variant POL-Filter. COL-Filter only indexes subscription queries but uses a score-oriented order for the inverted lists instead of query-oriented order in [21]. More precisely, a list for a query term τ indexes queries q containing τ, ordered by the ratio between the importance of τ in q and the current k-th best score for that q. This allows efficient top-k processing by using the TA algorithm on the index lists, but suffers from a relatively high number of updates subsequent to k-th best score changes. Message exit from the time sliding window also results in updates to the top-k results.

In a similar context, [24] proposes a strategy for sharing effort among queries in the top-k computation process, based on a covering relationship between subscription queries and an associated graph index, resulting in efficient top-k processing.

[28] proposes an adaptation of two IR top-k retrieval strategies to information streams: the document-at-a-time (DAAT) algorithm WAND [4] and the term-at-a-time (TAAT) algorithm of Buckley and Lewit [5]. Instead of time sliding windows, an continuous order-preserving decay function is proposed to handle time-dependent scoring, which eliminates the problem of top-k recomputing upon message expiration.

Unlike the above approaches considering text information streams with monotonic and homogeneous scoring functions, [29] introduces a simple social network factor in scoring: a global importance of each message, that may be based on social network criteria. This results in non-homogeneous scoring functions, where methods proposed by the approaches above are not applicable. They use a two-dimensional inverted query indexing scheme and explore efficient score bounds which drastic pruning of the search space. Like for [28], time-dependent scoring is handled through decay functions.

Excepting the last approach, all these continuous top-k processing techniques are limited to simple text scoring functions. We aim at extending these techniques to scoring functions including rich social network components.

3   Data Model and Scoring Function

As mentioned above, we consider the problem of continuously computing the k most important messages for each user in a social network, coming from information streams published by other users in the network.

We first propose a general social network model that covers many cases of popular social network environments. Then, based on this model, we propose a general scoring function for the importance of a published message relative to a given user.

3.1   Information Stream Social Networks

Definition 1. *An information stream social network S is a tuple $S = (U, R, p, sim, f, s)$, where:*

- *U is a set of users.*
- *$R = \{(u_1, u_2)|u_1, u_2 \in U, u_1 \neq u_2\}$ is a set of non-symmetric relations between users; $(u_1, u_2) \in R$ means that u_1 "follows" the messages published by u_2.*
- *$p : U \to \mathcal{D}$ is a function associating to each user a profile. User profiles and message contents are both modeled as descriptive documents in $\mathcal{D}$.*
- *$sim : \mathcal{D}^2 \to [0, 1]$ is a function measuring the similarity between two descriptive documents.*
- *$f : U^2 \to [0, 1]$ is a function associating to each couple of users (u_1, u_2) the importance of u_2 for u_1 in the social network.*
- *$s : U \to \mathcal{I}$ is a function associating to each user the information stream generated by that user.*

Note that U and R respectively define the nodes and edges of the directed social network graph. To represent symmetric networks such as Facebook, two edges must be created between any related nodes u_1 and u_2: (u_1, u_2) and (u_2, u_1).

The structure of descriptive documents in $\mathcal{D}$, which model both user profiles and message contents, depends on the nature of messages. Intuitively, the profile document gathers the elements of interest for the user in messages. In the common case of text messages, where similarity is evaluated through vector models like tf-idf, a descriptive document $d \in \mathcal{D}$ may be represented as a vector of terms belonging to a dictionary $\mathcal{T}$, with a tf-idf weight associated to each term, i.e. $d = \{(t, w) | t \in \mathcal{T}, w \in \mathbb{R}^+\}$.

At the same time, a user profile represents *the subscription query* for that user. For instance, users are interested in messages whose contents is relevant to their profiles.

The *sim* function measures the similarity between descriptive documents. For a message content mc and a user u, $sim(mc, p(u))$ measures the interest of user u (whose profile is $p(u)$) for message of content mc. For instance, the tf-idf similarity between documents d_1 and d_2 is measured by the cosine between their vectors of weights.

Note that the user relative importance function f is defined for any couple of users in the network graph, not only for those directly related through R. Like R, f is asymmetric, generally $f(u_1, u_2) \neq f(u_2, u_1)$. Depending on the context and on the design choices, the values of $f(u_1, u_2)$ may depend on many factors, such as the paths connecting u_1 to u_2 in the graph, the similarity of the two user profiles, the actions of u_1 on the messages of u_2, etc. Consequently, the values of f may vary in time, with the creation/deletion of users and relations, with profile changes, new interactions, etc.

The choice of introducing f as a global function, characterizing any couple of users, corresponds to our intention to go beyond locality in social network relationships. While in most social networks one only sees streams published by "friends" (users to which one is explicitly connected), we aim at providing users with both a *local view* (messages from the user's "community") and a *global one* (from the rest of the network).

The information streams published by users are defined as follows.

Definition 2. *An information stream $I \in \mathcal{I}$ is a couple $I = (M, A)$, where:*

- $M = \{(ts, mc) | ts \in TS, mc \in \mathcal{D}\}$ *is a set of messages, where ts is the timestamp of the message and mc is the descriptive document of the message contents.*
- $A = \{(ts, u, m, type, ac) | ts \in TS, u \in U, m \in M, type \in AT, ac \in \mathcal{D}\}$ *is a set of actions on the stream messages. ts is the action's timestamp, u the user that realized it, m the target message of the action, type its type among a set of predefined action types AT, and ac the descriptive document of the action contents.*

Stream messages and actions are implicitly ordered by their timestamps. Actions are always associated to a message and may have various types. Note that an action is not a message, even if some of them (e.g. comments, retweets) may be similar to messages in contents and in the way they are produced - all social networks provide the mechanisms to make this distinction. Examples of actions in the particular case of Twitter are retweets, replies, favorite marks on tweets, etc.

3.2 Scoring Function

In the context of an information stream social network S, the ranking of messages is driven by a scoring function that expresses the importance of a message for a user. We propose a general form of the scoring function, taking into account not only content-based factors, but also social network and time factors.

Note that we consider this scoring function *in the context of continuous top-k processing of social network information streams*. As shown in Sect. 2, existing work in the same context only considered simple scoring functions, with practically no social network components.

We propose here a complex scoring function, including social network factors, but still adapted to continuous top-k processing. We first present a general form for the scoring function, then we give in Sect. 4 some hints on how such scoring functions may be handled for continuous processing.

Definition 3 Scoring function. *For a user $u \in U$ and a message m published by another user $u_m \in U, u_m \neq u$, the scoring function score $: \mathcal{M} \times U \to \mathbb{R}_+$ expresses the importance of message m for user u and has the following general form:*

$$score(m, u) = \mathcal{F}_g(CS(m, u), SS(m, u)) \tag{1}$$

- *$CS(m, u)$ expresses the content similarity between the contents of m and the profile of u. In our information stream social network model, $CS(m, u) = sim(m.mc, p(u))$.*
- *$SS(m, u)$ expresses the importance of message m to user u in the social network context.*
- *$\mathcal{F}_g$ is a monotonic aggregation function combining the content-based and the social network scores.*

The social network scoring component may take into account both *user* related and *interaction* related factors in the social network.

$$SS(m, u) = \mathcal{F}_s(US(m, u), AS(m, u)) \tag{2}$$

The monotonic aggregation function $\mathcal{F}_s$ combines the partial scores given by the user-related factors ($US(m, u)$) and by the interaction-related factors ($AS(m, u)$).

The user-related scoring function $US(m, u)$ may itself take into account two kind of factors, related to the message publisher or to the relation between the publisher and the potential receiver.

$$US(m, u) = \mathcal{F}_u(UI(u_m), UR(u, u_m)) \tag{3}$$

Here, the $UI(u_m)$ component expresses the global importance of the message publisher u_m in the social network, while $UR(u, u_m)$ measures the importance of u_m for u. They are combined through the $\mathcal{F}_u$ monotonic aggregation function. Since in our information stream social network model the relative importance of users is measured by the f function, we may consider that $UR(u, u_m) = f(u, u_m)$. UI may be based e.g. on measures of influence in the social network, such as the Klout score.

Similarly, the interaction-related scoring function $AS(m, u)$ has a global part related to message m and a part giving the importance of the interactions with m from the perspective of user u.

$$AS(m, u) = \mathcal{F}_a(AI(m), AR(m, u)) \tag{4}$$

Here, $AI(m)$ expresses the importance of message m coming from the interaction it provoked globally in the network. $AR(m, u)$ measures the importance of the interactions with the message from the perspective of user u. Intuitively, an action on m is important for u if it is done by a user u_a important for u. AI and AR, combined through the $\mathcal{F}_a$ monotonic aggregation function, may be modeled by various functions, increasing with the number of actions on the message.

If we consider the common case of linear aggregation functions, expressed as positive weighted sums, Formulas 1–4 result into the following form for the scoring function, which gives a better overview of its various components:

$$score(m, u) = \alpha CS(m, u) + \beta_1 UI(u_m) + \beta_2 f(u, u_m) + \gamma_1 AI(m) + \gamma_2 AR(m, u) \tag{5}$$

Note that state-of-the-art proposals for continuous top-k processing only consider the CS component, excepting [29] which also includes the AI and UI components.

Definition 4 Time dependent scoring function. *For a message m published at time t_m, the variation in time of the importance of message m for user u is expressed by the time-dependent scoring function $tscore : \mathcal{M} \times U \times TS \rightarrow \mathbb{R}_+$ such that for any moment $t \geq t_m$:*

$$tscore(m, u, t) = score(m, u) \cdot TD(t - t_m) \tag{6}$$

- *$score(m, u)$ is the scoring function from Definition 3 and expresses the initial importance of message m for user u at moment t_m.*
- *$TD : \mathbb{R}_+ \rightarrow [0, 1]$ is a decreasing function such that $TD(0) = 1$. TD expresses the decrease in time of the importance of message m, by associating to each time duration since the message publishing, a decrease factor in $[0, 1]$. For instance $tscore(m, u, t_m) = score(m, u)$ and if $t_1 > t_2 \geq t_m$ then $tscore(m, u, t_1) \leq tscore(m, u, t_2)$.*

We make here the common choice of a message and user independent time function, which greatly facilitates message query processing, as illustrated in the next section.

Moreover, we only consider *order-preserving decay functions* for TD, i.e. functions which guarantee that the relative order of message scores is preserved in time. More precisely, an order preserving decay function TD guarantees that if at some moment t we have $tscore(m_1, u_1, t) \leq tscore(m_2, u_2, t)$, then $tscore(m_1, u_1, t') \leq tscore(m_2, u_2, t'), \forall t' > t$. Order-preserving decay functions facilitate continuous top-k processing by preserving in time the relative order of messages in the top-k lists.

In the particular case of a time dependent factor handled by *a sliding time window* of size w_t, $TD(d) = 1$ if $d \leq w_t$ and $TD(d) = 0$ when $d > w_t$. Note than in this case TD is not order-preserving, a message exiting the sliding time window becoming less important than any message still in the window.

4 Processing Model

The general scoring function for social network information streams given by Definition 3 and Formulas 1 to 4, or by its linear expression 5 provides a rich model for importance evaluation compared to the state-of-the-art methods. The general function may be instantiated in many ways, with an impact on the processing method. The description of a complete solution in a specific case is out of the scope of this paper, but we present here a general approach for continuous top-k processing with such a scoring model.

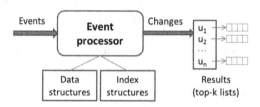

Fig. 1. General architecture for continuous top-k processing of information streams

Figure 1 presents the general architecture of continuous top-k processing of information streams, behaving as an event-based system. The result of such a process is the set of top-k messages for each user in the social network, continuously maintained by the system. The event processor handles every input event that may produce changes to the result lists, computes changes and subsequently updates the result lists. Change computation is based on the data structures representing the information streams and the social network, and on the index structures that enable efficient event processing.

In our information stream context, we distinguish two categories of events:

– *Continuously handled events*, with potentially strong impact on top-k update, and that must be processed on the spot. We include in this category, the publication of a new message and the interaction with an existing message.

– *Secondary events*, with a weaker impact on the top-k lists; they may be accumulated and processed from time to time. We include in this category changes in the social network that may produce small changes in the scoring parameters.

Evaluating the impact of various categories of events depending on the scoring model is a difficult problem, but continuously reacting to any event that may change some message score component is not realistic in practice, given the complexity of our scoring function. The above classification of events is a necessary trade-off between efficiency and precision.

Figure 2 presents the proposed architecture for continuous top-k processing of social network information streams with a scoring function such as (1). New message publishing and actions on messages are the only continuously handled events. They provoke a lookup in the index structures, composed of a content-based index and a social index. The result of this lookup is a subset of candidates for the top-k update. The role of the index is to drop from this candidate list as many users not impacted by the event as possible, in order to enable efficient top-k processing.

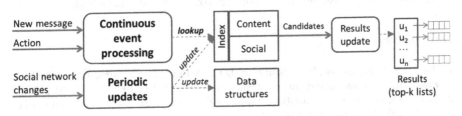

Fig. 2. Architecture for continuous top-k processing of social network information streams

Consider the linear form of the scoring function given by Formula 5 and let us note $\mu(u)$ the k-th score in the result list of user u. A new published message m has null score components for AI and AR (no action yet on m), so the only users u that must update their top-k list are those with $score(m, u) > \mu(u)$, i.e. with $e(u) = \alpha CS(m, u) + \beta_1 UI(u_m) + \beta_2 f(u, u_m) - \mu(u) > 0$. The design of the index structure must be based on the form of the $e(u)$ function.

In the case of a new action on message m, only the AI and AR components of the score change, i.e. $\Delta score(m, u) = \Delta AI(m) + \Delta AR(m, u)$. If for some user u, this score increase is enough go beyond $\mu(u)$ then m will enter the top-k list of u. The index structure must enable quick detection of users impacted by this score increase.

Secondary events are identified as social network modifications (new user relation, new user, profile update, etc.) that may modify the parameters of the social graph and implicitly of the scoring function, especially the relative importance function f. We consider that a periodic recomputation of the social network parameters is scheduled by the system. This operation will produce an update of the data and index structures.

The time-dependent scoring function (6) implies a continuous decrease in time of message scores, that cannot be handled in continuous top-k processing. We adopt the approach in [28,29] based on a strictly positive order-preserving decay functions. Instead of decreasing scores for old messages, order-preserving allows increasing scores for new messages, without changing the relative order of scores. By fixing an initial moment t_0 in the system, any new message m published at time t_m will have the score multiplied by a "time bonus" of $1/TD(t_m - t_0)$, which grows with t_m. With this approach scores do not vary with time anymore, which is compatible with continuous top-k processing.

5   Conclusion

This paper presented our vision on continuous top-k processing over information streams in a social network context. We proposed a general model of information streams social networks with a rich scoring function mixing content-based, user-based, interaction-based and time-based components. A general approach for continuous top-k processing in this context completes our contribution.

References

1. Aguilera, M.K., Strom, R.E., Sturman, D.C., Astley, M., Chandra, T.D.: Matching events in a content-based subscription system. In: PODC 1999, pp. 53–61 (1999)
2. Bahmani, B., Goel, A.: Partitioned multi-indexing: bringing order to social search. In: WWW 2012, pp. 399–408 (2012)
3. Bianchi, S., Felber, P., Gradinariu, M.: Potop-Butucaru: stabilizing distributed r-trees for peer-to-peer content routing. IEEE Trans. Parallel Distrib. Syst. **21**(8), 1175–1187 (2010)
4. Broder, A.Z., Carmel, D., Herscovici, M., Soffer, A., Zien, J.: Efficient query evaluation using a two-level retrieval process. In: CIKM 2003, pp. 426–434 (2003)
5. Buckley, C., Lewit, A.F.: Optimization of inverted vector searches. In: SIGIR 1985, pp. 97–110 (1985)
6. Callan, J.: Document filtering with inference networks. In: SIGIR 1996, pp. 262–269 (1996)
7. Dahimene, R., Du Mouza, C., Scholl, M.: Efficient filtering in micro-blogging systems: We won't get flooded again. In: Ailamaki, A., Bowers, S. (eds.) SSDBM 2012. LNCS, vol. 7338, pp. 168–176. Springer, Heidelberg (2012)
8. Das, G., Gunopulos, D., Koudas, N., Sarkas, N.: Ad-hoc top-k query answering for data streams. In: VLDB 2007, pp. 183–194 (2007)
9. Del Corso, G.M., Gullí, A., Romani, F.: Ranking a stream of news. In: WWW 2005, pp. 97–106 (2005)
10. Fabret, F., Jacobsen, H.A., Llirbat, F., Pereira, J., Ross, K.A., Shasha, D.: Filtering algorithms and implementation for very fast publish/subscribe systems. SIGMOD Rec. **30**(2), 115–126 (2001)
11. Fagin, R.: Combining fuzzy information: an overview. SIGMOD Rec. **31**(2), 109–118 (2002)

12. Gabrilovich, E., Dumais, S., Horvitz, E.: Newsjunkie: Providing personalized news-feeds via analysis of information novelty. In: WWW 2004, pp. 482–490 (2004)
13. Golab, L., Özsu, M.T.: Issues in data stream management. SIGMOD Rec. **32**(2), 5–14 (2003)
14. Haghani, P., Michel, S., Aberer, K.: The gist of everything new: Personalized top-k processing over web 2.0 streams. In: CIKM 2010, pp. 489–498 (2010)
15. Hmedeh, Z., Kourdounakis, H., Christophides, V., du Mouza, C., Scholl, M., Travers, N.: Subscription indexes for web syndication systems. In: EDBT 2012, pp. 312–323 (2012)
16. Hu, Y., Li, M., Li, Z., Ma, W.-Y.: Discovering authoritative news sources and top news stories. In: Ng, H.T., Leong, M.-K., Kan, M.-Y., Ji, D. (eds.) AIRS 2006. LNCS, vol. 4182, pp. 230–243. Springer, Heidelberg (2006)
17. Jones, K.S., Walker, S., Robertson, S.E.: A probabilistic model of information retrieval: development and comparative experiments. Inf. Process. Manage. **36**(6), 779–808 (2000)
18. Khodaei, A., Shahabi, C.: Social-textual search and ranking. In: International Workshop on Crowdsourcing Web Search, Lyon, France, April 17, 2012, pp. 3–8 (2012)
19. Maniu, S., Cautis, B.: Efficient top-k retrieval in online social tagging networks. CoRR, abs/1104.1605 (2011)
20. Mouratidis, K., Bakiras, S., Papadias, D.: Continuous monitoring of top-k queries over sliding windows. In: SIGMOD 2006, pp. 635–646 (2006)
21. Mouratidis, K., Pang, H.: Efficient evaluation of continuous text search queries. IEEE Trans. Knowl. Data Eng. **23**(10), 1469–1482 (2011)
22. Page, L., Brin, S., Motwani, R., Winograd, T.: The pagerank citation ranking: Bringing order to the web. Technical report, Stanford University (1999)
23. Pripužić, K., Žarko, I.P., Aberer, K.: Top-k/w publish/subscribe: Finding k most relevant publications in sliding time window w. In: DEBS 2008, pp. 127–138 (2008)
24. Rao, W., Chen, L., Chen, S., Tarkoma, S.: Evaluating continuous top-k queries over document streams. World Wide Web **17**(1), 59–83 (2014)
25. Rao, W., Fu, AW.-C., Chen, L., Chen, H.: Stairs: Towards efficient full-text filtering and dissemination in a dht environment. In: ICDE 2009, pp. 198–209 (2009)
26. Salton, G., Buckley, C.: Term-weighting approaches in automatic text retrieval. Inf. Process. Manage. **24**(5), 513–523 (1988)
27. Schenkel, R., Crecelius, T., Kacimi, M., Michel, S., Neumann, T., Parreira, J.X., Weikum, G.: Efficient top-k querying over social-tagging networks. In: SIGIR 2008, pp. 523–530 (2008)
28. Shraer, A., Gurevich, M., Fontoura, M., Josifovski, V.: Top-k publish-subscribe for social annotation of news. Proc. VLDB Endow. **6**(6), 385–396 (2013)
29. Vouzoukidou, N., Amann, B., Christophides, V.: Processing continuous text queries featuring non-homogeneous scoring functions. In: CIKM 2012, pp. 1065–1074 (2012)
30. Wang, C., Zhang, M., Ru, L., Ma, S.: Automatic online news topic ranking using media focus and user attention based on aging theory. In: CIKM 2008, pp. 1033–1042 (2008)
31. Wu, D., Li, Y., Choi, B., Xu, J.: Social-aware top-k spatial keyword search. In: MDM 2014, pp. 235–244 (2014)
32. Yan, T.W., Garcia-Molina, H.: Index structures for information filtering under the vector space model. In: ICDE 1994, pp. 337–347 (1994)

33. Yan, T.W., García-Molina, H.: Index structures for selective dissemination of information under the boolean model. ACM Trans. Database Syst. (TODS) **19**(2), 332–364 (1994)
34. Yan, T.W., Garcia-Molina, H.: The sift information dissemination system. ACM Trans. Database Syst. **24**(4), 529–565 (1999)
35. Yin, P., Lee, W.-C., Lee, K.C.K.: On top-k social web search. In: CIKM, pp. 1313–1316. ACM (2010)
36. Zhang, Y., Callan, J.: Maximum likelihood estimation for filtering thresholds. In: SIGIR 2001, pp. 294–302 (2001)

Information Discovery

Mining Frequent and Homogeneous Closed Itemsets

Ines Hilali[1,2], Tao-Yuan Jen[1], Dominique Laurent[1(✉)], Claudia Marinica[1], and Sadok Ben Yahia[2]

[1] ETIS Laboratory - ENSEA/UCP/CNRS, Cergy-Pontoise, France
ines.hilali@gmail.com, {jen,dlaurent,claudia.marinica}@u-cergy.fr
[2] Computer Science Faculty of Tunis, Tunis, Tunisia
sadok.benyahia@fst.rnu.tn
http://www-etis.ensea.fr,
http://www.fst.tn

Abstract. It is well known that when mining frequent itemsets from a transaction database, the output is usually too large to be effectively exploited by users. To cope with this difficulty, several forms of condensed representations of the set of frequent itemsets have been proposed, among which the notion of closure is one of the most popular.

In this paper, we propose a new notion of closure that takes into account, not only the support of itemsets, but also their homogeneity degree with respect to a given taxonomy. To this end, we introduce and study the notion of *frequent and homogeneous closed itemset* and we show in particular that knowing all frequent and homogeneous closed itemsets along with their supports and homogeneity degrees, allows to know all frequent and homogenous itemsets. Moreover, we propose a level wise algorithm for mining frequent and homogeneous closed itemsets.

Keywords: Data mining · Frequent itemsets · Closed itemsets · Similarity measures

1 Introduction

The data mining field appeared with the promise of providing tools and techniques to discover useful and beforehand unknown knowledge in large contexts. Among these techniques, one of the most known is the discovery of *association rules* that allows to find correlations between items appearing in a given context.

First approaches allowing the extraction of association rules were mainly based on the determination of frequent itemsets. In doing so, these approaches have two major disadvantages, namely, on the one hand, the very high number of frequent itemsets incurs a very high extraction cost and, on the other hand, the overwhelming quantity of derived association rules, among which many are redundant, makes it impossible for the end user to exploit these rules.

Consequently, extracting condensed representations is a milestone towards the emerging "knowledge extraction" field. To this end, several approaches were

© Springer International Publishing Switzerland 2016
D. Kotzinos et al. (Eds.): ISIP 2014, CCIS 497, pp. 51–65, 2016.
DOI: 10.1007/978-3-319-38901-1_4

interested in the extraction of a subset of the whole set of frequent itemsets, called *condensed representation*. Among all possible condensed representations, *exact* ones are of particular interest, because they allow for a lossless regeneration of all frequent itemsets, without accessing the underlying transaction set.

In the literature, the most well known exact condensed representations of frequent itemsets are known as closed itemsets [2,9,10,12], non-derivable itemsets [4] and essential itemsets [5]. In this paper, we focus on closed itemsets assuming that moreover, items are organized according to a given taxonomy. In this context, based on a similarity measure defined as in [8], homogeneity is seen as a semantic interestingness criterion for selecting relevant itemsets, as done in [7]. In our approach, we consider the task of mining frequent and *homogeneous* itemsets, and we further restrict this set by defining a new notion of closure that takes into account frequency *and* homogeneity of itemsets.

We emphasize that we show in this paper that homogeneity can be seen as an anti-monotonic constraint on itemsets. Therefore, our work is closely related to the numerous approaches published so far on mining constraint frequent itemsets (see [3] for a brief survey of this topic along with the introduction of more sophisticated constraints that are out of the scope of the present paper). In these approaches, the authors typically consider the general problem of mining frequent itemsets satisfying monotonic or anti-monotonic constraints. Contrary to these approaches where only frequency is associated with a closure, in our work, *each* of the two anti-monotonic constraints (namely frequency and homogeneity) is associated with its own closure, and these two closures are combined to produce a new one. This new closure is then shown to provide an exact condensed representation of the frequent homogeneous itemsets.

We also note that the notion of itemset homogeneity was already used in our previous work [6] in the context of association rules built up from non frequent items. However, to the best of our knowledge, no other work addresses the issue of mining frequent itemsets under a homogeneity constraint as we do in this paper. We illustrate our approach using the following example, considered throughout the paper as a running example.

Example 1. Let $\mathcal{I} = \{a_1, a_2, a_3, n_1, s_1, s_2, v_1\}$ be a set of items. We consider that these items are organized according to the taxonomy shown in Fig. 1. Intuitively, this means that a_1, a_2 and a_3 are three alcoholic beverages such that a_1 is a beer whereas a_2 and a_3 are wines, n_1 is a non alcoholic beverage, s_1 and s_2 are two seafood products and v_1 is a vegetable.

Using these items, transactions are pairs of the form (Tid, I) where Tid is an identifier and I a subset of $\mathcal{I}$. In our example, we consider a fixed set Δ of six transactions as shown in Table 1, where each row represents a transaction (Tid, I). For example, the first row of Table 1 displays a transaction τ identified by t_1 and whose items are a_1, a_2, a_3, s_1 and s_2. As a notational convenience, subsets of $\mathcal{I}$ are denoted by the concatenation of their elements. For instance the set $\{a_1, a_2, a_3, s_1, s_2\}$ is simply denoted by $a_1a_2a_3s_1s_2$.

Frequent itemset mining applied to Δ for a support threshold $\sigma = 50\%$ shows that the itemsets $I_1 = a_1a_2$ and $I_2 = a_1s_2$ are frequent since at least three

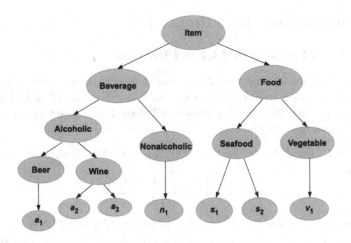

Fig. 1. The taxonomy T for the items in $\mathcal{I}$

Table 1. The set of transactions Δ of the running example

Tid	I
t_1	a_1, a_2, a_3, s_1, s_2
t_2	a_2, n_1, s_1
t_3	a_1, a_2, a_3, s_1, s_2
t_4	a_1, a_2, n_1, v_1
t_5	a_1, a_2, n_1, s_2, v_1
t_6	s_1, s_2, v_1

transactions contain these sets (t_1, t_3, t_4, t_5 contain I_1 and t_1, t_3, t_5 contain I_2). However, taxonomy T shows that items of I_1 are more similar to each other than are the items of I_2, that is, I_1 can be considered as *homogeneous*, contrary to I_2. Therefore, it is likely that users be more interested in I_1 than in I_2.   □

As earlier mentioned, in order to further reduce the size of the mined set, we introduce a new closure operator that combines the standard itemset closure [9] with one associated with homogeneity of itemsets. We show that mining closed itemsets according to this new closure operator allows to know, without accessing the dataset, *all* homogeneous and frequent itemsets. In other words, frequent and homogeneous closed itemsets form an exact condensed representation of frequent and homogeneous itemsets.

The paper is organized as follows: In Sect. 2 we first recall the basic notions related to frequent closed itemsets and then, we define *homogeneous* itemsets and their closure. In Sect. 3 we introduce our new notion of closure and then, in Sect. 4, we give an algorithm for computing all frequent and homogeneous closed itemsets. Section 5 concludes the paper and suggests future research issues.

2   Formalism and Basic Properties

2.1   Basics of Frequent and Closed Itemsets

In our approach, we assume a set $\mathcal{I}$ of items that occur in a transaction table Δ whose rows are called transactions. A transaction τ is a pair (Tid, I) where Tid is a transaction identifier and I a subset of $\mathcal{I}$, called an itemset and denoted by $It(\tau)$. We recall from [9] the following basic definition.

Definition 1. *Let I be an itemset. The support of I, denoted by $sup(I)$, is defined by:*

$$sup(I) = \frac{|\{\tau \in \Delta \mid I \subseteq It(\tau)\}|}{|\Delta|}.$$

Given a support threshold σ, I is said to be frequent, *if $sup(I) \geq \sigma$.*

The closure *of I with respect to Δ, or the Δ-closure of I, denoted by $\Gamma_\Delta(I)$, is defined by:*

$$\Gamma_\Delta(I) = \bigcap_{\tau \in \Delta, I \subseteq It(\tau)} It(\tau).$$

If I is such that $\Gamma_\Delta(I) = I$, then I is said to be Δ-closed.

It has been shown in [9] that

1. the support of an itemset I is equal to that of its Δ-closure, *i.e.*, $sup(I) = sup(\Gamma_\Delta(I))$, and that
2. the Δ-closure of I is the smallest Δ-closed itemset (with respect to set inclusion) that contains I.

As a consequence, for every itemset I, the support of I is equal to the support of the smallest Δ-closed itemset containing I. As noticed in [9], this property shows that mining all frequent Δ-closed itemsets and their support allows to compute all frequent itemsets and their support.

Example 2. In the context of Example 1, for $I = a_1n_1$, we have $sup(I) = \frac{2}{6}$ (since $I \subseteq It(t_4)$ and $I \subseteq It(t_5)$), and $\Gamma_\Delta(I) = It(t_4) \cap It(t_5) = a_1a_2n_1v_1$. Therefore, for a support threshold $\sigma = 25\%$, I is frequent but not Δ-closed. Moreover, since $sup(\Gamma_\Delta(I)) = \frac{2}{6}$, $\Gamma_\Delta(I)$ is a frequent and Δ-closed itemset.

On the other hand, for $I' = a_1n_1v_1$, $\Gamma_\Delta(I)$ is the least Δ-closed set containing I'. Therefore, we know, without any further computation, that $sup(I') = \frac{2}{6}$. $\qquad\square$

2.2   Homogeneous Itemsets

As earlier mentioned, interestingness of itemsets can be measured based not only on their frequency, but also on their *homogeneity*. Homogeneity is defined based on a taxonomy that is assumed to be defined over the items in $\mathcal{I}$. More precisely, we consider in this work that we are given a taxonomy T, a taxonomy being a tree whose leaves are the items in $\mathcal{I}$.

In this setting, we borrow from [11] the similarity measure between items called *Total Relatedness* and defined as a combination of two other partial similarity measures given next. In order to define these two measures, we assume that every node ν in T is associated with its *level*, denoted by $\lambda(\nu)$ and defined as usual, assuming that the level of the root of T is 0.

Definition 2. *Given two distinct items i and i' in $\mathcal{I}$, let* PATH(i, i') *be the set of internal nodes of the path in T connecting i and i'. The* Highest-Level Relatedness *and the* Node Separation Relatedness *are respectively defined as follows:*

- *The* Highest-Level Relatedness *of i and i', denoted by* HR(i, i'), *is the minimal level of the nodes in* PATH(i, i') *(or the level of the lowest common ancestor of i and i').*
- *The* Node Separation Relatedness *of i and i', denoted by* NSR(i, i'), *is the number of nodes in* PATH(i, i').

Denoting by k the depth of T, the Total Relatedness *measure is defined for all items i and i' in $\mathcal{I}$ by:*

$$sim(i, i') = \begin{cases} 1 & \text{if } i = i' \\ \frac{1 + \text{HR}(i, i')}{k * \text{NSR}(i, i')} & \text{otherwise.} \end{cases}$$

Example 3. In the context of Example 1, and considering the taxonomy over the items in $\mathcal{I}$ shown in Fig. 1, we have $k = 4$ and:

- HR$(a_1, a_3) = \lambda(\texttt{Alcoholic}) = 2$ and HR$(n_1, s_2) = \lambda(\texttt{Item}) = 0$,
- NSR$(a_1, a_3) = 3$ and NSR$(n_1, s_2) = 5$.

Therefore, according to Definition 2, we obtain:

- $sim(a_1, a_3) = \frac{1+2}{4*3} = 0.25$
- $sim(n_1, s_2) = \frac{1+0}{4*5} = 0.05$. □

The notion of homogeneity degree of an itemset is defined as follows.

Definition 3. *The* homogeneity degree *of a given itemset I, denoted by hom(I), is defined by:*

$$hom(I) = \begin{cases} 1 & \text{if } I = \emptyset \\ \min_{i, i' \in I}(sim(i, i')) & \text{otherwise.} \end{cases}$$

Given a homogeneity degree threshold h, I is said to be homogeneous *with respect to h if hom$(I) \geq h$.*

It is easy to see that for all i and i', we have $0 \leq sim(i, i') \leq 1$. Hence, for any similarity threshold h less than or equal to 1, singletons are homogeneous.

The following proposition shows that homogeneity is an anti-monotonic constraint on itemsets, in much the same way as frequency.

Proposition 1. *For all itemsets I_1 and I_2 if $I_1 \subseteq I_2$ then hom$(I_1) \geq$ hom(I_2).*

Proof. We first notice that for any itemset I possibly empty, we have $\emptyset \subseteq I$ along with $hom(\emptyset) \geq hom(I)$. Now, let I_1 and I_2 be nonempty itemsets such that $I_1 \subseteq I_2$. If i_1 and i'_1 are two items in I_1 such that $sim(i_1, i'_1) = \min_{i,i' \in I_1}(sim(i, i'))$, then i_1 and i'_1 also belong to I_2. Hence, $sim(i_1, i'_1) \geq \min_{i,i' \in I_2}(sim(i, i'))$, entailing that $\min_{i,i' \in I_1}(sim(i, i')) \geq \min_{i,i' \in I_2}(sim(i, i'))$ holds. Thus by Definition 3, we have $hom(I_1) \geq hom(I_2)$, and the proof is complete.

Therefore, Proposition 1 shows that homogeneous itemsets with respect to a given threshold h can be mined using a level wise algorithm such as Apriori ([1]). Another consequence of Proposition 1 is that the approach of [2] on Δ-closed homogeneous itemsets applies in our context. However, we improve upon this work by introducing a closure related to homogeneity and by combining this closure with the more standard Δ-closure recalled earlier.

2.3   Itemset Closure with Respect to a Taxonomy

In what follows, we denote by $N(T)$, respectively $L(T)$, the set of all nodes in T, respectively the set of all parent-child links in T. The closure of an itemset I with respect to T, or the T-closure of I for short, is defined as follows.

Definition 4. *For every itemset I, the* closure of I with respect to a taxonomy T, *or the T-closure of I, denoted by $\Gamma_T(I)$, is defined by:*

$$\Gamma_T(I) = \{i \in \mathcal{I} \mid (\exists \nu \in N(T))(\exists i' \in I)((\nu, i) \in L(T) \wedge (\nu, i') \in L(T))\}.$$

If the itemset I is such that $\Gamma_T(I) = I$, then I is said to be T-closed.

Example 4. Referring back to $I_1 = a_1 a_3$ and $I_2 = n_1 s_2$ of Example 3, we have:

- As a_3 is in I_1 and since $(\texttt{Wine}, a_3)$ and $(\texttt{Wine}, a_2)$ are in $L(T)$, a_2 is in $\Gamma_T(I_1)$. As a_1 has no sibling, we obtain $\Gamma_T(I_1) = a_1 a_2 a_3$.
- $\Gamma_T(I_2)$ contains all siblings of n_1 and s_2, that is: $\Gamma_T(I_2) = n_1 s_1 s_2$.

For $I_3 = a_1 a_2 a_3 n_1$, we obtain $\Gamma_T(I_3) = I_3$. Thus I_3 is T-closed.   □

According to Definition 4, the T-closure of an itemset I is the set of all siblings of the items in I (considering that an item i is its own sibling). The following proposition shows that Γ_T, operating over itemsets is a closure operator.

Proposition 2. *For all itemsets I and I', we have:*

1. $I \subseteq \Gamma_T(I)$
2. *If $I \subseteq I'$ then $\Gamma_T(I) \subseteq \Gamma_T(I')$*
3. $\Gamma_T(I) = \Gamma_T(\Gamma_T(I))$.

Proof. 1. This point follows immediately from Definition 4.
2. Let i be in $\Gamma_T(I)$. Denoting by ν the node such that (ν, i) is in $L(T)$, by Definition 4, I contains an item i' such that (ν, i') is in $L(T)$. Since $I \subseteq I'$, i' is a node of I', meaning that i is also a node in $\Gamma_T(I')$. Thus, $\Gamma_T(I) \subseteq \Gamma_T(I')$.

3. The previous two points imply that $\Gamma_T(I) \subseteq \Gamma_T(\Gamma_T(I))$ holds. Now, let i be in $\Gamma_T(\Gamma_T(I))$. In this case, denoting by ν_1 the node such that (ν_1, i) is in $L(T)$, $\Gamma_T(I)$ contains an item i_1 such that (ν_1, i_1) is in $L(T)$. Applying again the same argument to i_1, denoting by ν_2 the node such that (ν_2, i_1) is in $L(T)$, I contains an item i_2 such that (ν_2, i_2) is in $L(T)$. Since T is a tree, there exists a single node ν such that (ν, i_1) is in $L(T)$, and so, $\nu = \nu_1 = \nu_2$. Hence, i_2 is a node in I such that (ν, i_2) and (ν, i) are in $L(T)$. Consequently, i is in $\Gamma_T(I)$, which implies that $\Gamma_T(\Gamma_T(I)) \subseteq \Gamma_T(I)$. Therefore, the proof is complete.

The following proposition states that the T-closure of a union of two itemsets is the union of the T-closures of these itemsets.

Proposition 3. *For all itemsets I_1 and I_2, we have:*

$$\Gamma_T(I_1 \cup I_2) = \Gamma_T(I_1) \cup \Gamma_T(I_2).$$

Proof. For $j = 1, 2$, $I_j \subseteq I_1 \cup I_2$ implies that $\Gamma_T(I_j) \subseteq \Gamma_T(I_1 \cup I_2)$, by Proposition 2(2). Thus $\Gamma_T(I_1) \cup \Gamma_T(I_2) \subseteq \Gamma_T(I_1 \cup I_2)$ holds.

Conversely, if i is in $\Gamma_T(I_1 \cup I_2)$, then by Definition 4, $I_1 \cup I_2$ contains an item i' and $N(T)$ contains a node ν such that (ν, i) and (ν, i') are in $L(T)$. Thus, if i' is in I_1 (respectively in I_2), then applying again Definition 4, we obtain that i is also in $\Gamma_T(I_1)$ (respectively in $\Gamma_T(I_2)$). Therefore, $\Gamma_T(I_1 \cup I_2) \subseteq \Gamma_T(I_1) \cup \Gamma_T(I_2)$ holds, which completes the proof.

Now, comparing the homogeneity degree of an itemset with that of its T-closure, we give an example showing that these homogeneity degrees are *not* always equal. This is so because, in the context of Example 1, for $I = s_1$, we have $hom(I) = 1$, and $sim(\Gamma_T(I)) = sim(s_1, s_2) = \frac{1+2}{4*1} = 0.75$.

However, the following proposition states that, when I contains more than one item, the homogeneity degrees of I and $\Gamma_T(I)$ are equal.

Proposition 4. *For every non singleton itemset I, $hom(I) = hom(\Gamma_T(I))$.*

Proof. We first note that the result holds if $I = \emptyset$ because in this case, $\Gamma_T(I) = \emptyset$ and so by Definition 3, $hom(I) = hom(\Gamma_T(I)) = 1$.

Assume that $I \neq \emptyset$ and thus that I contains at least two distinct items. By Proposition 2(1) and Proposition 1, $hom(\Gamma_T(I)) \leq hom(I)$. Let i_1 and i_2 be distinct items in $\Gamma_T(I)$ such that $hom(\Gamma_T(I)) = sim(i_1, i_2)$ (these two items exist because I contains at least two elements i_1 and i_2 and because $sim(i_1, i_2) \leq sim(i_p, i_p)$ for $p = 1, 2$). By Definition 4, there exist two nodes ν_1 and ν_2 in T and two items j_1 and j_2 in I such that $(\nu_1, i_1), (\nu_1, j_1), (\nu_2, i_2), (\nu_2, j_2)$ are in $L(T)$.

On the other hand, if i and i' are distinct sibling items in T then for every item j we have $\text{HR}(i, j) = \text{HR}(i', j)$ and $\text{NSR}(i, j) = \text{NSR}(i', j)$, and thus $sim(i, j) = sim(i', j)$. Therefore, $sim(i_1, i_2) = sim(j_1, j_2)$. As Definition 3 implies that $hom(I) \leq sim(j_1, j_2)$, we obtain that $hom(I) \leq sim(i_1, i_2)$. Hence $hom(I) \leq hom(\Gamma_T(I))$, which shows that $hom(I) = hom(\Gamma_T(I))$. Therefore, the proof is complete.

As a consequence of Proposition 4, knowing all homogeneous T-closed itemsets along with their homogeneity degrees allows for knowing all homogeneous itemsets and their homogeneity degrees. Thus, homogeneous T-closed itemsets form an exact condensed representation of all homogeneous itemsets.

Referring back to Example 4, for $I_1 = a_1a_3$, as $\Gamma_T(I_1) = a_1a_2a_3$, we have $hom(I_1) = hom(a_1a_2a_3)$. Moreover, for $I = a_1a_2n_1$, we have $\Gamma_T(I) = a_1a_2a_3n_1 = I_3$. Thus, we know that $hom(I) = hom(I_3)$ without any further computation.

As for mining frequent *and* homogeneous itemsets or *FH-itemsets* for short, based on the fact that the support and homogeneity degree measures are anti-monotonic with respect to set inclusion (see Proposition 1), it turns out that FH-itemsets can be mined using a level wise algorithm such as Apriori ([1]). The corresponding algorithm is out of the scope of the present paper; instead we focus on a new notion of closure combining the Δ- and T-closures.

3   Frequent Homogeneous Closed Itemsets

3.1   The Problem

We know from the previous section that all frequent Δ-closed itemsets and all homogeneous T-closed itemsets allow to know all FH-itemsets. Thus, one would expect that the union of these two exact condensed representations be an exact condensed representation of the set of all FH-itemsets. However, the following example shows that this is *not* case.

Example 5. In the context of Example 1, with $\sigma = 40\%$ and $h = 20\%$, the set F_Δ of pairs $(I, sup(I))$ where I is a frequent Δ-closed itemset and the set H_T of pairs $(I, hom(I))$ where I is a homogeneous T-closed itemset are as follows:

$$F_\Delta = \{(a_1a_2, 0.66), (a_1a_2s_2, 0.5), (a_2, 0.83), (a_2n_1, 0.5), (a_2s_1, 0.5), (s_1, 0.66),$$
$$(s_1s_2, 0.5), (s_2, 0.66), (v_1, 0.5)\}$$
$$H_T = \{(a_1, 1), (a_1a_2a_3, 0.25), (a_2a_3, 1), (n_1, 1), (s_1s_2, 0.75), (v_1, 1)\}.$$

On the other hand, it can be seen that the computation of FH-itemsets gives the following set $FH(\Delta)$ of triples $(I, sup(I), hom(I))$:

$$FH(\Delta) = \{(a_1, 0.66, 1), (a_1a_2, 0.66, 0.25), (a_2, 0.83, 1), (n_1, 0.5, 1), (s_1, 0.66, 1),$$
$$(s_1s_2, 0.5, 0.75), (s_2, 0.66, 1), (v_1, 0.5, 1)\}.$$

We now argue that finding an exact condensed representation of $FH(\Delta)$, based on F_Δ and/or H_T is not trivial. Indeed, considering first $F_\Delta \cup H_T$ is not an option, because this union is clearly greater in size than $FH(\Delta)$. On the other hand, considering $F_\Delta \cap H_T$ is not an option either because, in our example, this would give s_1s_2 and v_1, which does not allow to recover $FH(\Delta)$.

Another way to cope with the problem of finding an exact condensed representation of $FH(\Delta)$ is to consider only those Δ-closed frequent itemsets that are homogeneous or dually, those T-closed homogeneous itemsets that are frequent. It has been stated in [2] that the first option is not correct, and in fact it turns out that the second one is also not correct. This is so in our example because:

- a_1a_2, a_2, s_1, s_1s_2, s_2 and v_1 are the only homogeneous Δ-closed itemsets and they do *not* allow to recover $FH(\Delta)$, since n_1 does not occur;
- a_1, n_1, s_1s_2 and v_1 are the only frequent T-closed itemsets and they do *not* allow to recover $FH(\Delta)$, since a_2 does not occur. □

3.2 ΔT-Closed Itemsets

In order to define an exact condensed representation of FH-itemsets, we introduce the notion of ΔT-*closure* as follows.

Definition 5. *Let Δ be a transaction table and T a taxonomy over $\mathcal{I}$. For every itemset I, the ΔT-closure of I with respect to Δ and T, or the ΔT-closure of I for short, denoted by $\Gamma_{\Delta T}(I)$, is defined by:*

$$\Gamma_{\Delta T}(I) = \Gamma_{\Delta}(I) \cap \Gamma_T(I).$$

If the itemset I is such that $\Gamma_{\Delta T}(I) = I$, then I is said to be ΔT-closed.

Example 6. To illustrate Definition 5, we consider again the context of Example 1 in which we compute the ΔT-closures of the itemsets occurring in $FH(\Delta)$, i.e., a_1, a_1a_2, a_2, n_1, s_1, s_1s_2, s_2, and v_1. Based on the results of Example 5, we have:

- $\Gamma_{\Delta}(a_1) = \Gamma_{\Delta}(a_1a_2) = \Gamma_{\Delta}(a_2) = a_1a_2$, and $\Gamma_T(a_1) = a_1$, $\Gamma_T(a_1a_2) = a_1a_2a_3$, $\Gamma_T(a_2) = a_2a_3$. Thus, $\Gamma_{\Delta T}(a_1) = a_1$, $\Gamma_{\Delta T}(a_1a_2) = a_1a_2$, $\Gamma_{\Delta T}(a_2) = a_2$.
- $\Gamma_{\Delta}(n_1) = a_2n_1$, and $\Gamma_T(n_1) = n_1$. Thus, $\Gamma_{\Delta T}(n_1) = n_1$.
- $\Gamma_{\Delta}(s_1) = s_1$, $\Gamma_{\Delta}(s_1s_2) = s_1s_2$, $\Gamma_{\Delta}(s_2) = s_2$, and $\Gamma_T(s_1) = \Gamma_T(s_1s_2) = \Gamma_T(s_2) = s_1s_2$. Thus, $\Gamma_{\Delta T}(s_1) = s_1$, $\Gamma_{\Delta T}(s_1s_2) = s_1s_2$, $\Gamma_{\Delta T}(s_2) = s_2$.
- $\Gamma_{\Delta}(v_1) = v_1$, and $\Gamma_T(v_1) = v_1$. Thus, $\Gamma_{\Delta T}(v_1) = v_1$.

Therefore, all itemsets in $FH(\Delta)$ are ΔT-closed. As an example of a non ΔT-closed itemset, consider $I = a_3s_1$. In this case, we have $\Gamma_{\Delta}(I) = It(t_1) \cap It(t_2) = a_1a_2a_3s_1s_2$ and $\Gamma_T(I) = a_2a_3s_1s_2$, and thus $\Gamma_{\Delta T}(I) = a_2a_3s_1s_2$. □

The following proposition shows that $\Gamma_{\Delta T}$, operating over itemsets is a closure operator.

Proposition 5. *For all itemsets I and I', we have:*

1. $I \subseteq \Gamma_{\Delta T}(I)$
2. *If $I \subseteq I'$ then $\Gamma_{\Delta T}(I) \subseteq \Gamma_{\Delta T}(I')$*
3. $\Gamma_{\Delta T}(I) = \Gamma_{\Delta T}(\Gamma_{\Delta T}(I))$.

Proof. 1. Since $I \subseteq \Gamma_{\Delta}(I)$ and $I \subseteq \Gamma_T(I)$ both hold, by Definition 5, we have $I \subseteq \Gamma_{\Delta T}(I)$.
2. If $I \subseteq I'$ then we have $\Gamma_{\Delta}(I) \subseteq \Gamma_{\Delta}(I')$ and $\Gamma_T(I) \subseteq \Gamma_T(I')$. Therefore, by Definition 5, we also have $\Gamma_{\Delta T}(I) \subseteq \Gamma_{\Delta T}(I')$.
3. According to the previous two items, we have that $\Gamma_{\Delta T}(I) \subseteq \Gamma_{\Delta T}(\Gamma_{\Delta T}(I))$. On the other hand, by Definition 5, $\Gamma_{\Delta T}(I) \subseteq \Gamma_{\Delta}(I)$ and so, $\Gamma_{\Delta T}(\Gamma_{\Delta T}(I)) \subseteq$

$\Gamma_{\Delta T}(\Gamma_\Delta(I))$ holds. Since $\Gamma_{\Delta T}(\Gamma_\Delta(I)) \subseteq \Gamma_\Delta(\Gamma_\Delta(I))$, we obtain $\Gamma_{\Delta T}(\Gamma_{\Delta T}(I)) \subseteq \Gamma_\Delta(\Gamma_\Delta(I))$, that is $\Gamma_{\Delta T}(\Gamma_{\Delta T}(I)) \subseteq \Gamma_\Delta(I)$ (because $\Gamma_\Delta(\Gamma_\Delta(I)) = \Gamma_\Delta(I)$). As it can be shown in a similar way that $\Gamma_{\Delta T}(\Gamma_{\Delta T}(I)) \subseteq \Gamma_T(I)$ also holds, we obtain $\Gamma_{\Delta T}(\Gamma_{\Delta T}(I)) \subseteq \Gamma_{\Delta T}(I)$, which completes the proof.

We now show that the support, respectively the homogeneity degree, of an itemset I and the support, respectively the homogeneity degree, of its ΔT-closure are equal, if I is not a singleton.

Proposition 6. *For every itemset I, $sup(I) = sup(\Gamma_{\Delta T}(I))$. Moreover, if I is a non singleton itemset, $hom(I) = hom(\Gamma_{\Delta T}(I))$.*

Proof. Since $I \subseteq \Gamma_{\Delta T}(I)$, $sup(I) \geq sup(\Gamma_{\Delta T}(I))$ and $hom(I) \geq hom(\Gamma_{\Delta T}(I))$ both hold. On the other hand, as $\Gamma_{\Delta T}(I) \subseteq \Gamma_\Delta(I)$, $sup(\Gamma_{\Delta T}(I)) \geq sup(\Gamma_\Delta(I))$. Since $sup(\Gamma_\Delta(I)) = sup(I)$ we obtain $sup(\Gamma_{\Delta T}(I)) \geq sup(I)$, and thus, $sup(I) = sup(\Gamma_{\Delta T}(I))$. Moreover, as $\Gamma_{\Delta T}(I) \subseteq \Gamma_\Delta(I)$, we also have $hom(\Gamma_{\Delta T}(I)) \geq hom(\Gamma_\Delta(I))$, by Proposition 1. As by Proposition 4, $hom(\Gamma_\Delta(I)) = hom(I)$ we obtain $hom(\Gamma_{\Delta T}(I)) \geq hom(I)$, and thus, $hom(I) = hom(\Gamma_{\Delta T}(I))$. Therefore, the proof is complete.

As a consequence of Proposition 6, the support and the homogeneity degree of a non singleton itemset I are respectively equal to the support and the homogeneity degree of the smallest ΔT-closed itemset that contains I. As a consequence, the knowledge of frequent homogeneous ΔT-closed itemsets along with their supports and homogeneity degrees allows for the computation of all FH-itemsets with their supports and their homogeneity degrees. In other words, frequent homogeneous ΔT-closed itemsets form an *exact condensed representation* of the set of all FH-itemsets. The computation of all frequent homogeneous ΔT-closed homogeneous itemsets, or *FH-ΔT-closed itemsets* for short, along with their supports and homogeneity degrees is the subject of the next section.

4   The Computation of FH-ΔT-Closed Itemsets

4.1 T-Elementary Itemsets

Definition 6. *An itemset I is said to be a T-elementary itemset if there exists a unique node ν in $N(T)$ such that $I = \{i \mid (\nu, i) \in L(T)\}$.*

Example 7. In the context of Example 1, it is easy to see that $I = a_2 a_3$ is a T-elementary itemset, because in T, (Wine, a_2) and (Wine, a_3) are the only links starting from Wine (see Fig. 1). We also notice that I is a T-closed itemset.

On the other hand, $I' = a_1 a_2 a_3$ is T-closed but I' is *not* a T-elementary itemset because (Beer, a_1) and (Wine, a_2) are links of $L(T)$.

Moreover, $I'' = a_1 a_2 a_3 s_2$ is an example of an itemset that is neither T-closed nor T-elementary. Indeed, the fact that $\Gamma_T(I'') = a_1 a_2 a_3 s_1 s_2$ shows that I'' is not T-closed, and the fact that (Beer, a_1) and (Wine, a_2) are links of $L(T)$ shows that I'' is not a T-elementary itemset.   □

It is easy to see that the computation of T-elementary itemsets is linear in the size of the set of items $\mathcal{I}$. The following proposition shows that T-elementary itemsets are the basic blocks from which T-closed itemsets are obtained.

Proposition 7. *1. If E is a T-elementary itemset then E is T-closed and for every subset I of E, $\Gamma_T(I) = E$.*
2. For every itemset I, $\Gamma_T(I)$ is the union of all T-elementary itemsets E such that $I \cap E \neq \emptyset$.

Proof. 1. If E is T-elementary, then, by Definition 6, E is the set of all nodes i such that (ν, i) is in $L(T)$ for a unique ν in $N(T)$. Therefore, by Definition 4, E is T-closed. Now, if $I \subseteq E$, then the items in I are all connected to the node ν, and so, we have $\Gamma_T(I) = E$.
2. We first notice that, since T is assumed to be a tree, the set of all T-elementary itemsets is a partition of $\mathcal{I}$. Consequently, for every itemset I, if $E_1, \ldots, E_k$ are all T-elementary itemsets such that $I \cap E_j \neq \emptyset$, for $j = 1, \ldots, k$, we have $I = (I \cap E_1) \cup \ldots \cup (I \cap E_k)$, implying that $\Gamma_T(I) = \Gamma_T((I \cap E_1) \cup \ldots \cup (I \cap E_k))$. Moreover, by Proposition 3, we have $\Gamma_T((I \cap E_1) \cup \ldots \cup (I \cap E_k)) = \Gamma_T(I \cap E_1) \cup \ldots \cup \Gamma_T(I \cap E_k)$. Since the previous item implies that $\Gamma_T(I \cap E_j) = I_j$, for $j = 1, \ldots, k$, we obtain that $\Gamma_T(I) = E_1 \cup \ldots \cup E_k$, which completes the proof.

Now, if E is a T-elementary itemset, all items in E have the same level in T, say λ. Thus, for all distinct items i and i' in E, we have $sim(i, i') = \frac{1+(\lambda-1)}{k*1}$, that is $sim(i, i') = \lambda/k$. Therefore, $hom(E) = \lambda/k$, showing that, depending on the homogeneity threshold h, some T-elementary itemsets may not be homogeneous. On the other hand, there exists at least one T-elementary itemset E_k whose elements are at level k (remember that k is the height of T). Thus, $hom(E_k) = 1$, meaning that there is at least one homogeneous T-elementary itemset.

Next, we propose an algorithm for computing all triples $(I, sup(I), hom(I))$ where I is an FH-ΔT-closed itemset; we denote by $FH_{\Delta T}$ this set.

4.2   An Algorithm for the Computation of $FH_{\Delta T}$

Our algorithm relies on the following well-known results regarding Δ-closure shown in [9].
    Given an itemset I, we denote by $Tr(I)$ the set of all transactions τ in Δ such that $I \subseteq It(\tau)$. Considering the equivalence relation whereby two itemsets I and I' are *equivalent* if $Tr(I) = Tr(I')$, the set of all equivalence classes thus defined is denoted by $Cl(\Delta)$. Now, if C is an equivalence class in $Cl(\Delta)$, we have:

1. The minimal itemsets in C are called the *key itemsets* of C. We denote by $K(C)$ the set of all key itemsets of C.
2. The union of all itemsets in C is also in C, and this union is precisely the Δ-closure of all itemsets in C. We denote by $\Gamma_\Delta(C)$ this Δ-closed itemset.
3. I is in C if and only if there is K in $K(C)$ such that $K \subseteq I \subseteq \Gamma_\Delta(C)$.
4. All itemsets in C have the same support, which we denote by $sup(C)$. Moreover, C is said to be frequent with respect to the threshold σ if $sup(C) \geq \sigma$.

Based on equivalence classes as recalled just above and T-elementary itemsets, ΔT-closed itemsets can be characterized as follows.

Proposition 8. *An itemset I is ΔT-closed if and only if there exists C in $Cl(\Delta)$ and T-elementary itemsets $E_1, \ldots, E_p$ such that the following three items hold:*

1. $I = (E_1 \cup \ldots \cup E_p) \cap \Gamma_\Delta(C)$.
2. *There exists K in $K(C)$ such that $K \subseteq I$.*
3. *For every $i = 1, \ldots, p$, $E_i \cap \Gamma_\Delta(C) \neq \emptyset$.*

Moreover, in case I is ΔT-closed, $sup(I) = sup(C)$ and if I is not a singleton then $hom(I) = hom(E_1 \cup \ldots \cup E_p)$.

Proof. Let $I = (E_1 \cup \ldots \cup E_p) \cap \Gamma_\Delta(C)$ be an itemset satisfying the items in the proposition. Then, I is an itemset in C and thus $\Gamma_\Delta(I) = \Gamma_\Delta(C)$. On the other hand, as T-elementary itemsets are pairwise disjoint, $E_1, \ldots, E_p$ are the only elementary itemsets that have a nonempty intersection with I. Therefore, by Proposition 7(2), $\Gamma_T(I) = E_1 \cup \ldots \cup E_p$. Thus, $\Gamma_{\Delta T}(I) = \Gamma_\Delta(I) \cap \Gamma_T(I) = I$, meaning that I is ΔT-closed. In this case, we have $sup(I) = sup(\Gamma_\Delta(I))$ and by Proposition 4, if I is not a singleton, $hom(I) = hom(E_1 \cup \ldots \cup E_p)$.

Conversely, let I be a ΔT-closed itemset. Then, there exists a class C such that I belongs to C, meaning that there exists K in $K(C)$ such that $K \subseteq I \subseteq \Gamma_\Delta(C)$. On the other hand, by Proposition 7(2), $\Gamma_T(I)$ is the union of all T-elementary itemsets $E_1, \ldots, E_p$ such that $E_i \cap I \neq \emptyset$ ($i = 1, \ldots, p$). Therefore, $\Gamma_{\Delta T}(I) = \Gamma_\Delta(C) \cap (E_1 \cup \ldots \cup E_p)$ and for $i = 1, \ldots, p$, $E_i \cap \Gamma_\Delta(C) \neq \emptyset$ (because $I \subseteq \Gamma_\Delta(C)$). Since $I = \Gamma_{\Delta T}(I)$, the three items in the proposition are satisfied by I, which completes the proof.

In our algorithm for computing FH-ΔT-closed itemsets, shown below as Algorithm 1, we rely on Proposition 8, assuming the following:

1. All homogeneous T-elementary itemsets and their homogeneity degrees have been computed beforehand. Let $HE(T)$ be the set of all pairs $(E, hom(E))$ such that E is a homogeneous T-elementary itemset.
2. All frequent equivalence classes of $Cl(\Delta)$ have also been computed along with their associated support. Let $FC(\Delta)$ denote the set of pairs $(C, sup(C))$ where C is a frequent class of itemsets.

We notice that in order to apply Proposition 8, key itemsets must be known, and that the approach in [9] does provide them. On the other hand, since the algorithms in [10] and in [12] do not compute key itemsets, considering one of these approaches implies extra computations. Whatever the way key itemsets are obtained, the two basic ideas of our algorithm are the following:

1. By Proposition 7, all homogeneous T-closed itemsets are generated through all unions of homogeneous elementary itemsets. These candidate unions are built up in a level wise manner and, thanks to Proposition 1, they are pruned as in Apriori ([1]) (lines 21 and 28).

Algorithm 1. Computation of FH-ΔT-closed itemsets

Input:
- The support threshold σ, the homogeneity degree threshold h, the taxonomy T
- The set $HE(T)$ of all pairs $(E, hom(E))$ where E is a homogeneous T-elementary itemset and $hom(E)$ its homogeneity degree
- The set $FC(\Delta)$ of all pairs $(C, sup(C))$ where $C = (K(C), \Gamma_\Delta(C))$ is a frequent equivalence class in $Cl(\Delta)$

Output: The set $FH_{\Delta T}$ of all triples $(I, hom(I), sup(I))$ where I is a frequent homogeneous ΔT-closed itemset

1: $FH_{\Delta T} = \emptyset$
2: $hom\text{-}union = \emptyset$
3: $hom\text{-}union\text{-}candidate = \{E \mid (E, hom(E)) \in HE(T)\}$
4: **for all** $(C, sup(C)) \in FC(\Delta)$ **do**
5:   **for all** E in $hom\text{-}union\text{-}candidate$ **do**
6:     **if** $E \cap \Gamma_\Delta(C) \neq \emptyset$ **then**
7:       $hom\text{-}union = hom\text{-}union \cup \{E\}$
8:       **if** $(\exists K \in K(C))(K \subseteq E)$ **then**
9:         **if** $E \cap \Gamma_\Delta(C)$ is a singleton **then**
10:           $hom\text{-}degree = 1$
11:         **else**
12:           $hom\text{-}degree = hom(E)$
13:         $FH_{\Delta T} = FH_{\Delta T} \cup \{(E \cap \Gamma_\Delta(C), hom\text{-}degree, sup(C))\}$
14: $first\text{-}loop = true$
15: **while** $hom\text{-}union \neq \emptyset$ **do**
16:   $hom\text{-}union\text{-}candidate = \emptyset$
17:   // Union candidate generation
18:   **if** $first\text{-}loop = true$ **then**
19:     **for all** $(E_1, hom(E_1))$ and $(E_2, hom(E_2))$ in $HE(T)$ **do**
20:       **if** $hom(E_1 \cup E_2) \geq h$ **then**
21:         $hom\text{-}union\text{-}candidate = hom\text{-}union\text{-}candidate \cup \{(E_1 \cup E_2)\}$
22:     $first\text{-}loop = false$
23:   **else**
24:     **for all** U_1 and U_2 in $hom\text{-}union$ **do**
25:       // $U_1 = E_1^1 \cup \ldots \cup E_1^{k-1}$, $U_2 = E_2^1 \cup \ldots \cup E_2^{k-1}$
26:       **if** $E_1^1 = E_2^1$ and ... and $E_1^{k-2} = E_2^{k-2}$ and $E_1^{k-1} \neq E_2^{k-1}$ **then**
27:         **if** for every subset I of $(U_1 \cup U_2)$ resulting from the union of $k-1$ sets among $E_1^1, \ldots, E_1^{k-1}$ and $E_2^1, \ldots, E_2^{k-1}$, I is in $hom\text{-}union$ **then**
28:           $hom\text{-}union\text{-}candidate = hom\text{-}union\text{-}candidate \cup \{(U_1 \cup U_2)\}$
29:   $hom\text{-}union = \emptyset$
30:   // Scan the set $FC(\Delta)$ and check the candidates in $hom\text{-}union\text{-}candidate$
31:   **for all** $(C, sup(C)) \in FC(\Delta)$ **do**
32:     **for all** $U = E^1 \cup \ldots \cup E^k$ in $hom\text{-}union\text{-}candidate$ **do**
33:       **if** $(\forall i = 1, \ldots, k)(E^i \cap \Gamma_\Delta(C) \neq \emptyset)$ **then**
34:         $hom\text{-}union = hom\text{-}union \cup \{U\}$
35:         **if** $(\exists K \in K(C))(K \subseteq U)$ **then**
36:           $FH_{\Delta T} = FH_{\Delta T} \cup \{(U \cap \Gamma_\Delta(C), hom(U), sup(C))\}$
37: **return** $FH_{\Delta T}$

---

2. The remaining candidate unions are checked according to the conditions in Proposition 8, considering the frequent equivalent classes of $FC(\Delta)$ (see lines 6-8 and lines 33-35).

Moreover, the following specific remarks are in order regarding Algorithm 1:

- The test line 20 can be performed by simply picking one item i_1 in E_1 and one item i_2 in E_2 and by computing $sim(i_1, i_2)$. This is so because E_1 and E_2 are elementary itemsets. This remark also holds in the more general case of a union of k elementary itemsets, when computing $hom(U)$, line 36.
- The test line 27 allows to consider only homogeneous candidate unions.
- The test line 35 allows to check whether $U \cap \Gamma_\Delta(C)$ belongs to C. Indeed, if the test succeeds, we have $K \subseteq U \cap \Gamma_\Delta(C) \subseteq \Gamma_\Delta(C)$ because $K \subseteq \Gamma_\Delta(C)$.
- Line 36, the homogeneity degree $hom(U \cap \Gamma_\Delta(C))$ is equal to $hom(U)$, because in this case, $U \cap \Gamma_\Delta(C)$ is not a singleton. Indeed, $U \cap \Gamma_\Delta(C)$ contains at least one item per elementary itemset occurring in U and in this case U is the union of at least two elementary itemsets.

As for the complexity of Algorithm 1, we first notice that the number of scans of $FC(\Delta)$ is linear in the size of $HE(T)$. Thus, the number of T-elementary itemsets clearly impacts the performance: in the worst case where all homogeneous T-elementary itemsets are singletons, the maximal number of scans of $FC(\Delta)$ is the number of items, and in the best case where we have only one homogeneous T-elementary itemset, only one scan of $FC(\Delta)$ is necessary.

In any case, since computing $HE(T)$ is linear in the size of $\mathcal{I}$, our approach to restrict itemsets to be frequent, homogeneous and ΔT-closed requires a computation in $O(|\mathcal{I}| \times |FC(\Delta)|)$ (where the notation $|E|$ stands for cardinality of set E).

Thus, considering that, in general, the size of $FC(\Delta)$ is much smaller than that of Δ, we claim that our approach does not incur a significant increase in complexity compared with that of mining frequent Δ-closed itemsets, using the method in [9]. However, it is important to notice that computing $FC(\Delta)$ using the method in [10] or in [12] requires to compute the key itemsets of every equivalence class. This clearly implies an additional cost whose evaluation is not considered in this paper.

5   Conclusion

In this paper, we have considered the problem of restricting the set of itemsets mined from a transaction table, using a semantic criterion based on a homogeneity measure for itemsets. In this context, we have introduced a novel notion of closure for itemsets, called ΔT-closure, that combines the well-known closure related to the support measure with a closure related to the notion of homogeneity degree of an itemset. We then could show that frequent homogeneous ΔT-closed itemsets form an exact condensed representation of the set of all frequent homogeneous itemsets. An algorithm for mining frequent homogeneous ΔT-closed itemsets has been proposed.

Regarding current and future work, we are implementing Algorithm 1, in order to assess its performance in terms of computational time as well as of its capability to actually condense the set of all frequent homogeneous itemsets. We are also investigating how to design a novel algorithm that would compute $FH_{\Delta T}$, without having to compute $FC(\Delta)$ first. Moreover, coupling this approach with that in [6] should provide a mean for deeply analyzing a given data set by considering frequent and non frequent homogeneous itemsets. This general issue will be investigated in the next future.

References

1. Agrawal, R., Mannila, H., Srikant, R., Toivonen, H., Verkamo, A.I.: Fast discovery of association rules. In: Advances in Knowledge Discovery and Data Mining, pp. 309–328. AAAI-MIT Press, (1996)
2. Bonchi, F., Lucchese, C.: On closed constrained frequent pattern mining. In: IEEE International Conference on Data Mining (ICDM), pp. 35–42 (2004)
3. Bonchi, F., Lucchese, C.: Pushing tougher constraints in frequent pattern mining. In: Ho, T.-B., Cheung, D., Liu, H. (eds.) PAKDD 2005. LNCS (LNAI), vol. 3518, pp. 114–124. Springer, Heidelberg (2005)
4. Calders, T., Goethals, B.: Mining all non-derivable frequent itemsets. In: Elomaa, T., Mannila, H., Toivonen, H. (eds.) PKDD 2002. LNCS (LNAI), vol. 2431, pp. 74–85. Springer, Heidelberg (2002)
5. Casali, A., Cicchetti, R., Lakhal, L.: Essential patterns: a perfect cover of frequent patterns. In: Tjoa, A.M., Trujillo, J. (eds.) DaWaK 2005. LNCS, vol. 3589, pp. 428–437. Springer, Heidelberg (2005)
6. Hilali, I., Jen, T.-Y., Laurent, D., Marinica, C., Ben Yahia, S.: Mining interesting disjunctive association rules from unfrequent items. In: Kawtrakul, A., Laurent, D., Spyratos, N., Tanaka, Y. (eds.) ISIP 2013. CCIS, vol. 421, pp. 84–100. Springer, Heidelberg (2014)
7. Marinica, C., Guillet, F.: Knowledge-based interactive postmining of association rules using ontologies. IEEE TKDE 22(6), 784–797 (2010)
8. Natarajan, R., Shekar, B.: A relatedness-based data-driven approach to determination of interestingness of association rules. In: ACM Symposium on Applied Computing (SAC), pp. 551–552. ACM (2005)
9. Pasquier, N., Bastide, Y., Taouil, R., Lakhal, L.: Discovering frequent closed itemsets for association rules. In: Beeri, C., Bruneman, P. (eds.) ICDT 1999. LNCS, vol. 1540, pp. 398–416. Springer, Heidelberg (1998)
10. Pei, J., Han, J., Mao, R.: Closet: an efficient algorithm for mining frequent closed itemsets. In: ACM SIGMOD Workshop on Research Issues in Data Mining and Knowledge Discovery, pp. 21–30 (2000)
11. Shekar, B., Natarajan, R.: A framework for evaluating knowledge-based interestingness of association rules. Fuzzy Optim. Decis. Making 3, 157–185 (2004)
12. Zaki, M.J., Hsiao, C.-J.: Efficient algorithms for mining closed itemsets and their lattice structure. IEEE TKDE 17(4), 462–478 (2005)

Mining Frequent Itemsets
with Vertical Data Layout in MapReduce

Tao-Yuan Jen, Claudia Marinica$^{(\boxtimes)}$, and Abir Ghariani

ETIS Laboratory, ENSEA/University of Cergy-Pontoise/CNRS 8051,
Cergy-Pontoise, France
{jen,claudia.marinica}@u-cergy.fr, abirghariani@gmail.com
http://www-etis.ensea.fr/

Abstract. Frequent itemset mining is a Data Mining technique aiming
to generate from a dataset new and interesting information under the
form of sets of items. Several algorithms were already proposed, and suc-
cessfully implemented and used such as *Apriori*, *FP-Growth* and *Eclat*,
along with numerous improvements. These algorithms deal with two
types of data layouts: horizontal and vertical; the former corresponds to
the traditional layout (the individuals as rows and the items as columns)
and it is more used due to its facility, but the latter brings important computation reductions. The standard frequent itemset mining algorithms
have a high computational complexity and, given the available massive
datasets, new approaches were proposed in the literature implementing
mining algorithms in parallel, distributed, and lately Cloud Computing
paradigms.

In order to overcome the drawbacks related to the computational issues,
in this paper, we propose, *Apriori_V*, a new parallel algorithm for frequent
itemset mining from a vertical data layout that was implemented on the
MapReduce platform. *Apriori_V* brings significant improvements related
to (1) the use of the vertical data layout with an *Apriori*-like strategy allowing to reduce the number of operations due to the elimination of several
Apriopri-specific tasks such as the pruning, and (2) decrease of the underlying complexity and thus the execution time.

Keywords: Data Mining · Association rules · MapReduce ·
Vertical/Horizontal data layout

1 Introduction

Data Mining is the process of providing interesting, unknown and potentially
useful patterns from data [8]. To this end, different techniques were developed
during the last decades. In this paper, we are interested in one of the most
used techniques, namely the frequent itemset (pattern) mining technique, which
allows the generation of correlations between items in the data.

Several algorithms along with numerous improvements were proposed in
order to extract frequent itemsets from data, such as *Apriori* [1], *FP-Growth* [9]

© Springer International Publishing Switzerland 2016
D. Kotzinos et al. (Eds.): ISIP 2014, CCIS 497, pp. 66–82, 2016.
DOI: 10.1007/978-3-319-38901-1_5

and *Eclat* [21]. On the one hand, *Apriori*, a level-wise algorithm, generates the complete set of frequent itemsets for a given dataset. When dealing with Big Data, *Apriori* encounters important difficulties related mainly to the dimension of the search space. More precisely, at each level $(k+1)$, the algorithm generates a huge number of candidate itemsets by joining the frequent itemsets produced at level k, and this number is growing exponentially. Moreover, at each level, *Apriori* needs to make one pass through the dataset in order to compute the support (i.e. the number of occurrences) of the candidate itemsets. On the other hand, a number of algorithms propose improvements by using different data structures. Some examples are the use of an *FP-Tree* structure in the *FP-Growth* algorithm, and the use of a vertical data layout (instead of the horizontal one used in *Apriori*) in *Eclat*-like algorithms. The vertical data layout has the advantage of cutting off several costly operations as candidate pruning and itemset support counting, since (as we will explain later in the paper) these become simple binary operations.

Despite the numerous existing solutions, in the BigData era, the main limitation of the frequent itemset mining technique is related to the complexity and the performance. To overcome these limits, new approaches were developed based on paradigms such as parallel, distributed or Cloud computing (which combines both parallel and distributed characteristics). Cloud Computing [2] promises access to unlimited number of resources and thus allows the design of algorithms that can scale as much as needed and take advantages of these resources (including CPU, storage and networking).

Cloud Computing brings in and supports different computational paradigms; one of these is MapReduce [6]. MapReduce provides a rather simple and easy to follow computational model, which benefits most repetitive computations that can be performed independently over various computational nodes. Frequent itemset mining algorithms that use the vertical data layout can be easily transformed to follow the requirements of MapReduce and thus to be executed under this framework. During the last years, various frequent itemset mining *Apriori*-like algorithms have been proposed on MapReduce. All these solutions are based on horizontal data layout. However they differ by the repartition of the tasks between the Mapper and the Reducer, and also by the number of MapReduce phases needed to produce a result.

In this context, this paper introduces a new algorithm, *Apriori_V*, aiming to reduce the computational complexity. The algorithm works on vertical data layouts and data are implemented as bitmaps in order to reduce numerous computations in level-wise mining algorithms based on horizontal data layout. To the best of our knowledge, no other *Apriori*-like algorithm using the vertical data layout and the bitmap representations was proposed over MapReduce. Moreover, we discuss a proposed MapReduce implementation for the new algorithm.

The reminder of the paper is structured as follows. Section 2 details the background for our problem - discussions about frequent itemset mining, MapReduce and frequent itemset mining on MapReduce are developed. In Sect. 3 we describe our algorithm, and we discuss its advantages/drawbacks in Sect. 4. Section 5 concludes our paper and brings up diverse perspectives.

2 Background: Frequent Itemset Mining, MapReduce and Related Work

2.1 Frequent Itemset Mining

Let $\Delta = \{t_1, t_2, ..., t_n\}$ be a dataset that contains n transactions, each transaction being composed of a subset of the set of items of the dataset $\mathcal{I} = \{i_1, i_2, ..., i_m\}$. A transaction $t_i \in \Delta$ is a pair (Tid, I), where Tid is the unique identifier of the transaction, and I is a set of items, $I \subseteq \mathcal{I}$, called also itemset.

Let $X = \{i_1, i_2, ..., i_k\}$ be an itemset; to facilitate the reading, we denote X by $X = i_1 i_2 ... i_k$. The itemset X is supported by the transaction $t_i = (Tid, I)$, if X is a subset of I, $X \subseteq I$, or more precisely, if the transaction t_i contains the itemset X. With these elements, we are able to define the support of an itemset.

Definition 1. *The support of an itemset X, denoted by $sup(X)$, is the ratio of transactions containing X over the total number of transactions in the dataset:*

$$sup(X) = \frac{|\{t_i = (Tid, I) \in \Delta \mid X \subseteq I\}|}{|\Delta|}.$$

Definition 2. *Given a minimum support threshold, σ, specified by the user, an itemset X is frequent if its support exceeds the given threshold ($sup(X) \geq \sigma$).*

Given these basic notions, the main issue in the frequent itemset mining research area is to develop algorithms generating *all* the frequent itemsets from a dataset given a minimum support threshold. We illustrate our approach using the following example considered throughout the paper as a running example.

Example 1. Let $\mathcal{I} = \{a, b, c, f, m, p\}$ be a set of items and Δ a dataset of 6 transactions as shown in Table 1.

In this table, each row represents a transaction (Tid, I). For example, the first row of Table 1 displays the transaction identified by t_1 and whose items are a, c, f, m and p.

Table 1. The set of transactions Δ of the running example.

Tid	I
t_1	a, c, f, m, p
t_2	a, b, c, f, m
t_3	b, f
t_4	b, c, p
t_5	a, c, f, m, p
t_6	a, c, f, m

Applying a standard technique to mine frequent itemsets from the transactional table Δ using a minimum support threshold $\sigma = 30\,\%$, the itemsets ac and bc are frequent since at least two transactions contain these sets. However, the itemset ab is not frequent since only the transaction t_2 contains the itemset ab.

Apriori. One of the most known and used algorithms for frequent itemset mining is the *Apriori* algorithm [1], a level-wise algorithm based on candidate generation. It performs a breadth-first search through the search space of all itemsets by iteratively generating candidate itemsets C_{k+1} of size $k + 1$ from the frequent itemsets L_k of size k. The anti-monotonicity condition imposes that an itemset is a candidate if all its sub-itemsets are frequent; then, to validate the candidate as frequent its support should be computed in the dataset.

More precisely, at first level ($k = 1$), the algorithm generates the set of candidates C_1 consisting of all the items in $\mathcal{I}$, and then it computes their support by one pass in the dataset. At level ($k + 1$), the algorithm generates candidates C_{k+1} in two steps: (1) first, in the join step, the union of two frequent itemsets of level k produces an itemset; (2) second, in the pruning step, the generated itemsets are validated as being candidates if they satisfy the anti-monotonicity property. At the end, the support of all the candidates of level ($k+1$) is computed by one pass in the dataset.

2.2   The MapReduce Platform

MapReduce is a platform introduced in 2004 by Dean and Ghemawat from Google [5] and it showed massive adoption and implementation by both industrial and scientific circles [4,6]. The most prominent implementation of the MapReduce framework is Hadoop[1]. Hadoop is the framework we retained for the implementation of our new algorithm. MapReduce is a rather simple computational framework but converting existing algorithms to MapReduce is not always a strightforward process. Many times actually new MapReduce-only algorithms should be proposed due to the difficulty of transforming the old ones.

MapReduce is based on the splitting of the given algorithm in two phases; (1) the *Mapper* or the Mapping phase and (2) the *Reducer* or Reducing phase. All nodes in the MapReduce framework are expected to run the exact same code, so we can only differentiate the input. In that respect, MapReduce belongs to the Single Instruction Multiple Data (SIMD) parallel computing class of frameworks. But before starting the actual MapReduce processing, we have to take a step into splitting the input adequately and as equally as possible. The latter is required so that the nodes running the processing for the Mappers will be expected to finish around the same time, since, according to MapReduce, moving to the Reduce phase is allowed only after all Mappers have finished and reported their results. Moreover, during this preprocessing phase, we need to convert the input to trivial *(key, value)* pairs, since MapReduce relies on processing as input and producing as output only (key, value) pairs. How this transformation will take place depends on the current problem.

After the preprocessing phase, the Mapping phase starts, where usually a set of semi-processing computations on the input takes place. After the Mapping phase, a sorting/shuffling takes place in order to prepare the intermediate results produced by the Mappers for processing by the Reducers. Usually the effort is to pro-

---

[1] https://hadoop.apache.org/.

vide to the Reducers input that is somehow related, e.g. by using the same key. Then, the Reducers will do the final computations over the already semi-processed dataset and produce the final results in the form of new (key, value) pairs.

2.3 Frequent Pattern Mining on MapReduce

During the last decade, an important number of algorithms for frequent pattern mining have been developed in the literature. As stated previously, due to the limits of these algorithms related to memory use and computation cost, solutions were further searched in the parallel and distributed computing, and lately in Cloud Computing (using specific implementations such as Hadoop or Spark[2]) with the development of different approaches [16].

In the following, we will focus on the algorithms for frequent itemset mining developed on the MapReduce platform and we can classify them in 3 categories depending on the number of MapReduce phases needed to accomplish the task: (1) one-phase; (2) two-phases; and (3) k-phases algorithms, where k is the maximum length of the frequent itemsets produced by the algorithm.

One-Phase Algorithms. The algorithms in the one-phase category need only one MapReduce job to accomplish the task. The algorithm proposed in [12] has a reduced efficiency as it has to produce many redundant itemsets. As a consequence, while applied on Big Data, the algorithm leads to memory overflow, high CPU utilization and high execution time.

Algorithm 1. Mapper for the one-phase algorithm in [12]

Input: S_i where
    S_i: *Split* number i and *line = transaction*
Output: $(Key, 1)$ where
    Key: a candidate itemset
 1: **for all** transactions t in S_i **do**
 2:    Map(*line* offset, t)
 3:    **for all** itemsets I in t **do**
 4:       **return** $(I,1)$;

For this algorithm, the Mapper is given in Algorithm 1 and the Reducer in Algorithm 2. We can see that, from a given transaction t, each Mapper is producing all the possible itemsets along with the value 1. Then, for each itemset generated by the Mapper, the Reducers are computing its occurrence in the database. At the end, the Reducers are testing each itemset's support against the given threshold and returns the frequent item sets with their corresponding support.

---

[2] https://spark.apache.org/.

Algorithm 2. Reducer for the one-phase algorithm in [12]

Input: $(Key_2, Value_2)$ pairs and min_sup, where
    Key_2: a candidate itemset
    $Value_2$: Key_2's occurrence in each split
Output: $(Key_3, Value_3)$ pairs, where
    Key_3: an element of frequent itemsets
    $Value_3$: $Key_3's$ occurrence in the whole data
1: $Sum = 0$;
2: **while** $Value_2.hasNext()$ **do**
3:    $Sum+ = Value_2.getNext()$;
4: **if** $Sum >= min\_sup$ **then**
5:    **return** (Key_2, Sum);

Algorithm 3. Mapper for the 1st job of the *MRApriori* algorithm [18]

Input: S_i where
    S_i: *Split* number i and $line = transaction$
Output: $(Key, 1)$ where
    Key: a partial frequent k-itemset
    $Value$: Key's partial occurence
1: $L = apply\_Apriori\_on(S_i)$
2: **for all** itemsets I in L **do**
3:    **return** $(I, $ partial count$)$;

Algorithm 4. Mapper for the 1st job of the *MRApriori* algorithm [18]

Input: $(Key_2, Value_2)$ pairs, where
    Key_2: a partial frequent k-itemset
    $Value_2$: Key_2's occurrence in each split
Output: $(Key_3, 1)$ pairs, where
    Key_3: a global candidate frequent k-itemset
    $Value_3$: 1
1: **return** $(Key_2, 1)$;

Two-Phases Algorithms. The algorithms in this category need at maximum two MapReduce jobs to find the frequent itemsets and they work as follows:

1. In the first MapReduce job, each Mapper receives as input a part of the dataset and the goal of the Mapper is to apply on the input the *Apriori* algorithm with a minimum support threshold proportional to the dimension of the input.

    Thus, the output of the Mapper is composed of the a partial frequent k-itemset and its partial count. The Reducer receives as input the Mapper's output and generates as output the pair composed of each partial frequent itemset and the value 1. For this first job, the Mapper is given in Algorithm 3 and the Reducer in Algorithm 4.

2. The goal of the second MapReduce job is to compute the exact support for all the partial frequent itemsets. This second job is composed of the Mapper given in Algorithm 5 and the Reducer in Algorithm 6.

Each Mapper receives the same input as in the first job, but also the complete set of partial frequent itemsets generated by the first phase's Reducer, and it will compute the occurrence of all the partial frequent itemsets on the part of the database received as input. Then, the Reducer is will addition all the occurrences produced by the Mappers for an itemset in order to produce the final support.

Algorithm 5. Mapper for the 2nd job of the *MRApriori* algorithm [18]

Input: S_i, L_p
Output: $(Key, Value)$ where
    Key: an element of L_p
    $Value$: is Key's partial occurence in the split
1: Read L_p from $DistributedCache$
2: **for all** itemset I in L_p **do**
3:    Map(I, S_i)
4:    $count = Count\_I\_in\_S_i(I, S_i)$;
5:    **return** $(I, count)$;

Algorithm 6. Mapper for the 2nd job of the *MRApriori* algorithm [18]

Input: $(Key_2, Value_2)$ pairs, where
    Key_2: a global candidate k-itemset
    $Value_2$: Key_2's occurrence in each split
Output: $(Key_3, Value_3)$ pairs, where
    Key_3: a global frequent k-itemset
    $Value_3$: Key_3's global occurrence in the whole data
1: $Sum = 0$;
2: **while** $Value_2.hasNext()$ **do**
3:    $Sum+ = Value2.getNext()$;
4: **if** $Sum >= min\_sup$ **then**
5:    **return** (Key_2, Sum)

The *MRApriori* algorithm [18] follows the above steps, but it suffers from redundant count computation between the two phases. Indeed, in the second phase the authors compute the counts for all the partial frequent itemsets in all the splits, even for those being frequent in a specific split. More precisely, in the first phase, an itemset can be frequent in one split, and not frequent in the others, but this does not mean that it cannot be frequent in the global dataset.

To overcome this drawback, the algorithm *IMRApriori* [7] proposes to enhance the performances of the *MRApriori* algorithm by introducing an efficient pruning technique based on reducing the number of partial frequent itemsets. To reduce the overload nodes of the map functions, the *IMRApriori* prunes in the first phase's Reducer those itemsets that are not declared as frequent by a minimum number of Mappers. Other improvements for the *MRApriori* were proposed in [10,17], the latter introducing a cache layer in order to save the counting information in the first phase and to access it in the second phase.

k-phases Algorithms. The algorithms in the k-phases category need k MapReduce jobs to generate the frequent itemsets (k is the maximum length of the frequent itemsets). These algorithms bring different translations of the *Apriori* algorithm over the MapReduce platform. The algorithm introduced in [19] integrates at each k-phase a MapReduce job working as follows: (1) the k candidates are computed; (2) the Mapper receives as input a specific transaction and its goal is to output the pair composed of the candidate itemset and the value 1, if the candidate is included in the transaction; (3) the Reducer sums up all the values for each candidate itemset computing the support of the candidate.

Algorithm 7. Phase-1's Mapper of SPC and DPC algorithms [14]

Input: transaction t_i
    database partition D_i
Output: (*Key*, *Value*) where
    Key: an item in t_i
    Value: 1
1: **for all** transaction $t_i \in D_i$ **do**
2:    **for all** item $i \in t_i$ **do**
3:       **return** $(i, 1)$;

Improvements of the previous algorithm, such as [13,14], were developed, the latter introducing three algorithms that share the same first two phases:

- In the first phase, the Mapper (Algorithm 7) receives as input a transaction and it generates the 1-itemsets with the value 1. Based on that, the Reducer (Algorithm 8) computes the support for the 1-itemsets and prunes the not frequent ones.
- In the second phase, the Mapper (Algorithm 9) receives as input the same transaction as in the first phase, but it also has access to the list of frequent 1-itemsets. Based on these information, the Mapper will produce all the candidates 2-itemsets which will be verified against the support by the Reducer (Algorithm 10).

For the third phase and more, the first algorithm, *Single Pass Counting (SPC)* (see Algorithm 11), proposes to generate k-itemsets following the same strategy as in the first two phases. The two other algorithms have a different approach. On the one hand, an algorithm computes, in a phase grater than 2, the candidate itemsets of three levels at the same time (e.g. in the phase three, candidate 3-, 4- and 5-itemsets will be computed). On the other hand, *Dynamic Passes Combined-counting (DPC)* algorithm computes, in a phase greater than 2,

Algorithm 8. Phase-1's Reducer of SPC and DPC algorithms [14]

Input: $(Key_2, Value_2)$ pairs, where
    Key_2: a candidate 1-itemset
    $Value_2$: 1
Output: $(Key_3, Value_3)$ pairs, where
    Key_3: a frequent 1-itemset
    $Value_3$: Key_3's global occurrence in the whole data
1: $count = 0$;
2: **for all** v in $Value_2$ **do**
3:    $count+ = v$;
4: **if** $count >= min\_sup$ **then**
5:    **return** $(Key_2, count)$

Algorithm 9. Phase-k's Mapper of SPC and DPC algorithms [14]

Input: transaction t_i
    database partition D_i and L_{k-1} $(k >= 2)$
Output: $(Key, Value)$ where
    Key: a candidate itemset of level k
    $Value$: 1
1: read L_{k-1} from DistributedCache
2: construct a hash-tree for $C_k = apriori - gen(L_{k-1})$;
3: **for all** transaction $t_i \in D_i$ **do**
4:    $C_t = subset(C_k, t_i)$
5:    **for all** candidate $c \in C_t$ **do**
6:      **return** $(c, 1)$;

Algorithm 10. Phase-k's Reducer of SPC and DPC algorithms [14]

Input: $(Key_2, Value_2)$ pairs, where
    Key_2: a candidate 2-itemset
    $Value_2$: value list for Key_2
Output: $(Key_3, Value_3)$ pairs, where
    Key_3: a candidate 2-itemset
    $Value_3$: $Key_3's$ global occurrence in the whole data
1: $count = 0$;
2: **for all** v in $Value_2$ **do**
3:    $count+ = v$;
4: **if** $count >= min\_sup$ **then**
5:    **return** $(Key_2, count)$

---

candidate itemsets of a number of level previously computed using statistics on nodes' overload.

3   Apriori_V Algorithm

In this section, we introduce the *Apriori_V* algorithm, an *Apriori*-like algorithm on vertical data layouts working on the MapReduce platform.

Algorithm 11. Algorithm SPC [14]

Input: database
Output: List L of frequent itemsets
 1: Phase-1: find L_1 using the Mapper and the Reducer for Phase-1
 2: Phase-2: find L_2 using the Mapper and the Reducer for Phase-k where $k = 2$
 3: **for all** $k = 3$; L_{k-1} not empty set; $k + +$ **do**
 4:     Mapper (Phase-k)
 5:     Reducer (Phase-k)

3.1 Horizontal vs. Vertical Data Layout

In this section, we discuss two principal data layouts to store transactional data: *horizontal* and *vertical layout*. On the one hand, in the *horizontal data layout*, a dataset is stored as a set of (Tid, I) pairs. Each transaction is identified by the transaction identifier Tid and it contains the list I of items. On the other hand, in the *vertical data layout*, a dataset is organized as a set of $(Item, Bitmap)$ pairs, where the *Bitmap* is a binary representation of the transactions. In the *Bitmap*, one bit corresponds to each transaction and is set to 1 if the *Item* is contained in that transaction, and to 0 otherwise. For example, the dataset in Example 1 is presented in vertical data layout in Table 2. The bitmap in the first line shows that the transactions t_1, t_2, t_5 and t_6 contain the item a (value 1 in the bitmap), and that transactions t_3 and t_4 do not contain item a (value 0 in the bitmap). Consequently, the support of a can be computed as the number of bits of value 1 in the bitmap.

Table 2. The vertical data layout representation of the running example.

Item	$Bitmap(t_1, t_2, t_3, etc.)$
a	110011
b	011100
c	110111
f	111011
m	110011
p	100110

The main advantage of using vertical data layout in frequent itemset mining is to simplify the tasks of pruning and subset-finding when the traditional level-wise algorithms verify the frequency of the candidate itemsets. More precisely, frequent itemsets can be counted via the (bitwise) logical *AND* operation between bitmaps, instead using complex hash/search tree structures as in the horizontal approaches. It is also important to outline that in this case candidate generation and counting tasks take place in a single step. For example, if the itemsets ab and ac are frequent, mining algorithms on the vertical data layout can make a logical *AND* operation on their bitmaps to verify whether *abc* is a frequent itemset or not [11]. We will provide more of details related to this point later in the paper.

In the literature, several frequent itemset mining algorithms using a vertical data layout were proposed such as *Eclat* [21], *Diffset* [20], *VIPER* [15] and *MAFIA* [3], and also an implementation of *Eclat* over the MapReduce platform [22]. In the latter, the authors propose to execute the *Eclat* algorithm on each MapReduce node. It is important to outline that Eclat and *Apriori* algorithms differ in their (1) input dataset layout and (2) strategy to explore the search space. For the second point, *Apriori* uses a breath-first strategy, while *Eclat* uses a depth-first strategy. In this paper, our goal is to propose an algorithm with a vertical data layout input and using a breath-first strategy. The motivation is that this algorithm will allow computational reduction due to the fact that some operations required in *Apriori*-like algorithms are not compulsory when using input data in vertical layout.

3.2 *Apriori_V* Algorithm

In this section, we introduce the *Apriori_V* algorithm, a level-wise algorithm that mines all the frequent itemsets from a vertical dataset. Since most of datasets are organized in an horizontal layout, a data transformation from horizontal to vertical layout is necessary while preparing the dataset for the mining task. Moreover, verifying that an item is frequent in a vertical dataset equals to counting the number of bits set to 1 in its own bitmap. Hence, we propose to include the task of computing the frequent itemsets of level $k = 1$ in the data preparation phase, and the algorithm starts the MapReduce phases with the mining of frequent 2-itemsets.

Apriori_V algorithm is developed on the MapReduce platform and, in order to provide all the frequent itemsets, it needs a number of MapReduce jobs equal to the length of the largest frequent itemset generated minus one. For example, if from a given dataset, the largest frequent itemset that can be extracted has 5 items, the *Apriori_V* algorithm needs 4 MapReduce jobs to produce the result. Indeed, as stated above, the 1-itemsets are computed in the preparation phase. The operations preformed in each MapReduce job are the same and they are detailed below.

In the following discussion, we will detail the operations performed by the Mapper and Reducer in order to generate the set of $(k + 1)$-itemsets; thus, it is important to recall that we consider that all the itemsets of level less or equal to k were already generated in the previous $k - 1$ MapReduce jobs.

The Mapper. At level $(k + 1)$ we consider as known the set L_k of k-itemsets generated in the previous MapReduce job. In this context, the MapReduce system distributes to each Mapper a frequent k-itemset I as well as the list L_k^I of frequent k-itemsets whose $(k - 1)$ prefix is the same as I's $(k - 1)$ prefix. These two elements are sent to the Mapper as the *Key*. At the same time, the system also sends to each Mapper the corresponding bitmap of I as the *Value* of *Key*.

Algorithm 12. Mapper of the Apriori_V algorithm

Input: $Key, Value$ where
$\quad$ Key: (a k-itemset I,
$\qquad$ the list L_k^I of k-itemsets with the same $(k-1)$ prefix as I)
$\quad$ $Value$: the bitmap B of I
Output: a list of $(Key', Value')$ where
$\quad$ Key': set of candidate $(k+1)$-itemsets generated using I - C_{k+1}^I
$\quad$ $Value'$: the bitmap B of I
1: $C_{k+1}^I = \emptyset$
2: **for all** X in L_k^I **do**
3: $\quad$ **if** $X \neq I$ **then**
4: $\qquad$ $C_{k+1}^I = C_{k+1}^I \cup \{(X \cup I, B)\}$
5: **return** C_{k+1}^I

As shown in Algorithm 12, after receiving the input information, each Mapper generates the candidate $(k+1)$-itemsets using the frequent k-itemset I and, from left to right, one of the different frequent k-itemsets in L_k^I, named here X. This generation works as the candidate generation in the Apriori algorithm. For example, if $L_k^I = \{abc, abd, abe\}$ and $I = abd$, then, in this step, the Mapper will generate the candidate 4-itemsets $\{abcd, abde\}$. The output of the Mapper consists in the pair $(X \cup I, Bitmap\ of\ I)$, where $X \cup I$ is the Key and $Bitmap\ of\ I$ the $Value$.

The Reducer. Algorithm 13 shows the functioning of the Reducer that is detailed in the following. For the level $(k+1)$, each Reducer takes as input (1) as Key a specific candidate $(k+1)$-itemset I generated by the Mappers, and (2) as $Value$ the two bitmaps generated by the Mappers for the same candidate itemset and that correspond to the bitmap of the two itemsets used in the Mapper to generate I.

Each Reducer executes a logical AND operation on the two bitmaps in order to set on 1 these transactions containing I. A function $Count()$ counts the number of bits of value 1 in the resulted bitmap in order to get the support of I. If I is frequent (support greater or equal to a given threshold), then the Reducer returns it with the computed bitmap and support to the system for mining the next level frequent itemsets.

The mining procedure terminates when no frequent itemsets are returned by Reducers.

Example 2. In Fig. 1, we illustrate the mining process of the frequent 3-itemsets (minimum support threshold is set to $minsup = 30\%$) from the running example dataset. In the following, we consider that the set of frequent 2-itemsets, L_2, was generated by the first MapReduce job:

$$L_2 = \{ac, af, am, ap, bc, bf, cf, cm, cp, fm, fp, mp\}.$$

As pointed out earlier, first the system distributes to Mapper1 the itemset $I = ac$, the list $L_2^I = (ac, af, am, ap)$, and the I's bitmap 110011. We would like to

Algorithm 13. Reducer for Apriori_V

Input: Key, $Value$ where
$\quad$ Key: a candidate $(k+1)$-itemsets I
$\quad$ $Value$: B_1 and B_2, the bitmaps of the two itemsets the Mapper used previously to
$\quad$ generate I
Output: $(Key', Value')$ where
$\quad$ Key': $(I$, the bitmap B' of $I)$
$\quad$ $Value'$: the support Sup of I
1: $\quad B' = AND(B_1, B_2)$
2: $\quad$ // $Count()$ gets the number of bits containing value 1 in B'
3: $\quad Sup = Count(B')$
4: $\quad$ **if** $Sup \geq minsup$ **then**
5: $\quad\quad$ **return** $((I, B'), Sup)$
6: $\quad$ **else**
7: $\quad\quad$ **return**

---

mention that all frequent 2-itemsets having the same prefix a are included in the
list L_2^I. The Mapper1 generates the candidate 3-itemsets $C_3^I = \{acf,\ acm,\ acp\}$
by combining $I = ac$ with each 2-itemsets in L_2^I except itself. Moreover, if we
consider that Mapper1, Mapper2, Mapper3 and Mapper4 are dealing with the
same prefix a, then the list L_2^I sent with the itemset I to Mapper1 will also
be sent to the other 3 Mappers with, respectively, the itemsets af, am and
ap. These four Mappers and only these four Mappers generate all candidate
3-itemsets with the prefix a.

The bitmap 110011 of itemset $I = ac$ means that the transactions t_1, t_2,
t_5, and t_6 contain the itemset I. With the itemsets in C_3^I, this bitmap will be
sent to different Reducers as it is needed in order to compute the support of
candidate 3-itemsets. In Fig. 1, Reducer1 gets the bitmap 110011 of the itemset
ac and the bitmap 110011 of the itemset af to compute the support of the
candidate itemset acf (we can note that here the two bitmaps are aqual by
simple coincidence). Finally, Reducer1 sends necessary information to the system
for mining the frequent 4-itemsets in the next step since the result bitmap 110011
of the previous computing shows that the transactions t_1, t_2, t_5 and t_6 contain
the itemset acf and, hence, acf is a frequent itemset.

If we analyze the Mapper10 and the Mapper11 given in Fig. 1, we can note
that they produce the 3-level item sets with the prefix fm and fp. The Mapper10
will generate the itemset fmp with the bitmap 110011 corresponding to fm,
and the Mapper11 will generate the same itemset with the bitmap 100001 of fp.
The Reducer11 will apply the logical AND operation on these two bitmaps and
compute the support of the fmp itemset.

4   Discussion on Complexity and Performance

In this section, we will discuss the complexity of the $Apriori\_V$ algorithm in order
to be able to assess its performance. In order to compute the complexity, we recall

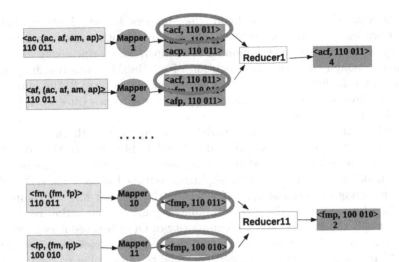

Fig. 1. The frequent 3-itemsets mining in *Apriori_V* with *minsup* = 30 %.

that the algorithm is applied on a dataset with m items and n transactions; also, we consider that k refers to the current level in the algorithm (as for Apriori), and *max_width* stands for the length of the largest frequent itemsets. As detailed in the previous section, the *Apriori_V* algorithm needs *max_width* $- 1$ MapReduce jobs to generate all frequent itemsets. In the following, we will discuss Mapper's and, respectively, Reducer's complexity at level $(k + 1)$.

Each Mapper receives a k-itemset I, the set of k-itemsets sharing the same $(k - 1)$ prefix with I, L_k^I, and I's bitmap. It is important to outline that the maximum cardinality of the L_k set is equal to k-combinations of m elements C_m^k, the maximum cardinality of the L_k^I set is m, as only the last item can change, and the bitmap of an itemset has n bits. Firstly, we can note that the best case is met when the number of Mappers is equal to $|L_k|$, knowing that the set of frequent itemsets is large at level 2, but after level 2 it starts decreasing. Secondly, the operations performed by the Mapper should produce the set of candidates C_{k+1}^I by combining the itemset I with each itemset in L_k^I (except I). As the cardinality of L_k^I is m, then the complexity of the Mapper is equal to $O(m)$.

Each Reducer receives a candidate from the set C_{k+1} and two bitmaps, all generated by the Mapper. The maximum cardinality of the set C_{k+1} is equal to $(k + 1)$-combination of m elements C_m^{k+1}, which implies that the best case is met when the number of Reducers is equal to $|C_{k+1}|$, but, as for the set of frequent itemsets, the set of candidates decreases also with the level. On the other hand, the operations performed by the Reducer implies a logical *AND* operation between the two bitmaps and then counting the 1 values in order to provide the support. In consequence, the complexity of Reducer's operations is equal to $O(n)$.

As a conclusion, on the one hand, the Mappers and the Reducers have a linear complexity on m, and respectively, n. On the other hand, to keep the linearity of the complexity, the number of Mappers and, respectively, Reducers should be enough to allow the execution of all the Map function in parallel (the same for Reducer); this issue is less obvious as, at level 2, the number of candidates/frequent itemsets is important and equal to $m * (m - 1)/2$, but it's decreasing in the next levels.

We decided to compare our algorithm's complexity with the one of the algorithm *Single Pass Counting* (SPC) developed in [14]; we chose SPC algorithm for comparison as it's the closest to ours in terms of number of MapReduce jobs and methodology. In short, the SPC algorithm, outlined in Sect. 2.3, is described by the following elements at level $(k + 1)$: (i) the Mapper has the complexity of $O(|L_k|)$ because it checks every candidate against a transaction received in the input; (ii) the Reducer has the complexity of $O(n)$ because it can receive a maximum of n entries for a candidate; (iii) the best case is met when the system has n Mappers and a number of Reducers equal to the number of candidates at each level.

Given these elements, we can conclude that (i) the Mapper's complexity of our algorithm is slightly lower than the one of the SPC algorithm; and (ii) the number of Mappers needed in our algorithm is bigger than in the SPC algorithm. Nevertheless, increasing the number of Mappers in a Cloud/MapReduce environment is an easier task than having to deal with highly demanding computations in the Mapper.

5   Conclusions and Future Work

In this paper we introduced a new algorithm for mining frequent itemsets, *Apriori_V*. *Apriori_V* is a level-wise frequent itemset mining algorithm based on vertical data layout and implemented on MapReduce. The advantages of this approach is that it does not need an additional structure, such as the tree structure in depth-first mining algorithms, to guide the mining procedure, and it also simplifies the pruning and subset-finding tasks.

For the immediate future, we plan to complete the implementation and experimental evaluation of the algorithm using a Hadoop based infrastructure. We also plan to work on reducing the amount of data transformed in data pre-processing/distribution step of the MapReduce jobs at the beginning of each level. Moreover, as the mining task of each level cannot start until the last level mining work has completely terminated producing some unnecessary waiting time, we plan to introduce a dynamic combination of several phases in one phase. Finally, we plan to experiment with very large data sets to evaluate the scalability of the algorithm.

Acknowledgements. We would like to gratefully thank Dimitris Kotzinos (ETIS - ENSEA/University of Cergy-Pontoise/CNRS 8051) for his contributions and support during this work.

References

1. Agrawal, R., Srikant, R.: Fast algorithms for mining association rules in large databases. In: Proceedings of the 20th International Conference on Very Large Data Bases, VLDB, pp. 487–499. Morgan Kaufmann Publishers Inc., San Francisco (1994)
2. Armbrust, M., Fox, A., Griffith, R., Joseph, A.D., Katz, R., Konwinski, A., Lee, G., Patterson, D., Rabkin, A., Stoica, I., Zaharia, M.: A view of cloud computing. Commun. ACM **53**(4), 50–58 (2010)
3. Burdick, D., Calimlim, M., Gehrke, J.: Mafia: a maximal frequent itemset algorithm for transactional databases. In: Proceedings of the 17th International Conference on Data Engineering, pp. 443–452. IEEE Computer Society, Washington DC (2001)
4. Chu, C.-T., Kim, S.K., Lin, Y.-A., YuanYuan, Y., Bradski, G.R., Ng, A.Y., Olukotun, K.: Map-reduce for machine learning on multicore. In: Advances in Neural Information Processing Systems 19, Proceedings of the Twentieth Annual Conference on Neural Information Processing Systems, Vancouver, 4–7 December 2006, pp. 281–288 (2006)
5. Dean, J., Ghemawat, S.: Mapreduce: simplified data processing on large clusters. In: OSDI, pp. 137–150. USENIX Association (2004)
6. Dean, J., Ghemawat, S.: Mapreduce: simplified data processing on large clusters. Commun. ACM **51**(1), 107–113 (2008)
7. Farzanyar, Z., Cercone, N.: Efficient mining of frequent itemsets in social network data based on mapreduce framework. In: Proceedings of the IEEE/ACM International Conference on Advances in Social Networks Analysis and Mining, ASONAM 2013, pp. 1183–1188. ACM, New York (2013)
8. Fayyad, U.M., Piatetsky-Shapiro, G., Smyth, P.: Advances in Knowledge Discovery and Data Mining. From Data Mining to Knowledge Discovery: An Overview. American Association for Artificial Intelligence, Menlo Park (1996)
9. Han, J., Pei, J., Yin, Y., Mao, R.: Mining frequent patterns without candidate generation: a frequent-pattern tree approach. Data Min. Knowl. Discov. **8**(1), 53–87 (2004)
10. Huang, D., Song, Y., Routray, R., Qin, F.: Smartcache: an optimized mapreduce implementation of frequent itemset mining. In: IEEE International Conference on Cloud Engineering (IC2E) (2014)
11. Jen, T.-Y., Taouil, R., Laurent, D.: A dichotomous algorithm for association rule mining. In: 15th International Workshop on Database and Expert Systems Applications (DEXA 2004), with CD-ROM, 30 August–3 September, Zaragoza, pp. 567–571 (2004)
12. Li, L., Zhang, M.: The strategy of mining association rule based on cloud computing. In: Proceedings of the International Conference on Business Computing and Global Informatization, BCGIN 2011, pp. 475–478. IEEE Computer Society, Washington DC (2011)
13. Li, N., Zeng, L., He, Q., Shi, Z.: Parallel implementation of apriori algorithm based on mapreduce. In: 2012 13th ACIS International Conference on Software Engineering, Artificial Intelligence, Networking and Parallel Distributed Computing (SNPD), pp. 236–241, August 2012
14. Lin, M.-Y., Lee, P.-Y., Hsueh, S.-C.: Apriori-based frequent itemset mining algorithms on mapreduce. In: Proceedings of the 6th International Conference on Ubiquitous Information Management and Communication, ICUIMC, pp. 76:1–76:8. ACM, New York (2012)

15. Shenoy, P., Haritsa, J.R., Sudarshan, S., Bhalotia, G., Bawa, M., Shah, D.: Turbo-charging vertical mining of large databases. In: Proceedings of the ACM SIGMOD International Conference on Management of Data, SIGMOD 2000, pp. 22–33. ACM, New York (2000)
16. Singh, S., Garg, R., Mishra, P.K.: A comparative study of association rule mining algorithms on grid and cloud platform. International Assoc. Sci. Innov. Res. (IASIR) **2** (2014)
17. Wang, L., Feng, L., Zhang, J., Liao, P.: An efficient algorithm of frequent itemsets mining based on mapreduce. J. Inf. Comput. Sci. **11**, 2809–2816 (2014)
18. Yahya, O., Hegazy, O., Ezat, E.: An efficient implementation of apriori algorithm based on hadoop-mapreduce model. Int. J. Rev. Comput. **12**, 59–67 (2012)
19. Yang, X.Y., Liu, Z., Yan, F.: Mapreduce as a programming model for association rules algorithm on hadoop. In: 3rd International Conference on Information Sciences and Interaction Sciences (ICIS), pp. 99–102, June 2010
20. Zaki, M.J., Gouda, K.: Fast vertical mining using diffsets. In: Proceedings of the Ninth ACM SIGKDD International Conference on Knowledge Discovery and Data Mining, KDD, pp. 326–335. ACM, New York (2003)
21. Zaki, M.J., Parthasarathy, S., Ogihara, M., Li, W.: New algorithms for fast discovery of association rules. Technical report, Rochester, NY, USA (1997)
22. Zhang, Z., Ji, G., Tang, M.: Mreclat: an algorithm for parallel mining frequent itemsets. In: Proceedings of the International Conference on Advanced Cloud and Big Data, CBD 2013, pp. 177–180. IEEE Computer Society, Washington DC (2013)

Knowledge Management Applications
on the Web and the Cloud

Webble World 3.0

In the Borderland Between Being a User or a Developer

Micke Kuwahara[✉] and Yuzuru Tanaka

Meme Media Laboratory, Hokkaido University, Sapporo, Japan
{mkuwahara,tanaka}@meme.hokudai.ac.jp

Abstract. Webble World 3.0 is the latest and most advanced and accessible of the meme media implementations, which allow users to fully participate in the process of building the next generation of the Web. Allowing the users of the World Wide Web to design and develop interactive building blocks for wrapping web resources, which then anyone may combine and use in any way imaginable. One important goal is to put the mainly passive web user in the driving seat and with this tool make him or her feel empowered to actively engage in building the web of our shared need and joy, but also to attract skilled web developers to work in a more modeled and collaborative environment.

Keywords: Webble · Meme media objects · Customize · Configure · Web · Share · Distribute · Resource · Interact · Participate · Federation · HTML5 · Tool · Software development

1 Introduction

Webbles are based on the philosophy of memes [3, 4], that every thought and knowledge shared by humans may collide with other thoughts and knowledge and then reproduce or mutate, all in favor of survival and adaptation. The meme is a paraphrase which is supposed to make us see that human knowledge and cultural expressions are like genes in the way they evolve.

1.1 IntelligentPad

The idea of the meme has stimulated the research on how to make human digital knowledge fit the meme description so that creativity may easier spread, evolve and enhance in a shared environment. One of these attempts was done by Tanaka and his group at Hokkaido University which gave us the theoretical as well as the practical creation of the IntelligentPad [1, 2, 5–7]. The purpose of this IntelligentPad, this meme media, is to work as smart containers of digital knowledge that may freely be connected and disconnected in arbitrary ways to form any imaginable compound object. Such an object can be anything digitally available in a computer today, from simple web blocks of images and textboxes to more complex gadgets and even full featured applications.

© Springer International Publishing Switzerland 2016
D. Kotzinos et al. (Eds.): ISIP 2014, CCIS 497, pp. 85–96, 2016.
DOI: 10.1007/978-3-319-38901-1_6

1.2   History

During the 1990s several IntelligentPad implementations were made, even one developed by the Japanese company Fujitsu. The latest were developed in the early 2000 and goes by the name 'Plexware' and is still in use in some commercial projects in Japan. All these systems were limited to desktop pc only though and possibilities to share pads were very limited.

In the beginning of 2008 began the development of a new type of IntelligentPad system that would be accessible online via an ordinary web browser. The end result saw the light of day around 2010, now under a new name called 'Webble World' and the pads were now Webbles. This version was developed using the early version of Microsoft Silverlight and required a free browser plugin provided by Microsoft to work. But it was very powerful in comparison to previous versions, especially when it came to form, shape and design of the individual Webbles.

The Silverlight plugin evolved and increased in power so in order to keep up, in 2012 Webble World 2.0 followed, and soon thereafter 2.5, together with a wide range of Webbles to help users and developers to create tools, games and web applications. This version is still available and actively used, though no longer maintained and improved upon.

But the Silverlight plugin had many faults. The first and foremost problem was the fact that it was a plugin and required users to install it before Webble World could work, something which could not be done satisfyingly on Mac, not at all on Linux and never on smart phones or tablets. Alongside with that, Silverlight became less and less maintained by Microsoft and the eminent feeling that it would be deprecated became more and more apparent to the community of Silverlight users.

Therefore in the summer of 2013, the development began to solve all these problems, by creating a new version of Webble World, version 3.0.

1.3   A Webble Under the Hood

Before getting into detail of what Webble World 3.0 is and what it can do, let's clarify what a 'Webble' really is.

The Concept. A Webble is the latest-generation Meme Media object, available inside a web-browser. It can be developed by a programmer within ordinary software development restrictions. When it has been deployed to the web it can be downloaded into the browser via a specialized web site by any Internet user together with other Webbles and combined together to form new compound Webbles which the user can configure so that they may solve some tasks, or present some content the user wants to share. Many such compound Webbles can also be combined as a larger and more complex Webble application. Webbles evolves step by step every time it gets reused and republished. Advanced web application development can be done, without additional programming, directly in the browser with these building blocks of 'meme Lego', called Webbles [8–10].

The Design. The Model-View-Controller structure is an essential part of the internal design of the Webble and fully supported by current (latest) implementation. In the previous version this was implemented by creating a separate model-module which was more a virtual model than a real one, while in this version we exploit the natural design of the AngularJS framework we use (see Sect. 2.2 – Client Side) which separates the controller into a JS-file (named controller.js) and the View which, naturally, is the HTML file (with support of CSS) named view.html. The model is the internal variables and the core code which the system inserts in each Webble, with main focus on slot management (see below).

A Webble can be or contain anything its creator wants, but in order to be called a Webble there are two things it must be able to have; relationships and slots.

Parent - Child relationship is how you structure the Webbles together. A child can only have one parent but a parent can have unlimited children.

Slots are where a Webble store its properties which can be configured and shared. The name slot is pointing out, that the outside world and other Webbles can plug into the value for various purposes (Fig. 1).

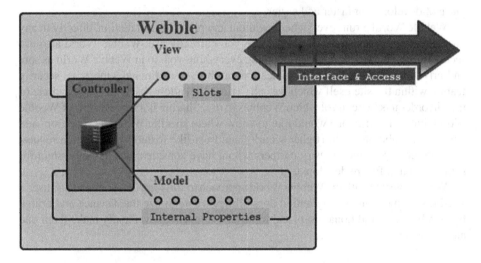

Fig. 1. Simplicity is the main focus in Webble design

With these basic features the Webble can be used to create complex applications within Webble World.

2   Webble World 3

Webble World 3 is a web-based federation of Webbles, which comes as building blocks, software tools, applications and entertainment widgets that can be used, configured, combined, altered, disassembled and improved etc. by any user at will.

2.1 Main Features

What we want to achieve with Webble world is a platform where users finds software, tools and interactive data the same way one would "Google" for information today. But also, within the same environment, allows the user to add, build, change and improve upon the system and the repository, with minimal skill-requirements. By the power of re-usage and shared resources, as well as the Webble's power to wrap most web content we hope that web apps can be built at a much more higher rate and less effort and also by ordinary people with little or no programming skills.

As a developer one can interact either by building core Building blocks (known as templates) with traditional web scripting, directly in the browser, or by building Webble software with the Webble World Interface by combining and configuring those mentioned building blocks with no scripting or programming.

Webble World has high focus on sharing and collaboration, in order to make each piece of development faster and easier.

Webble World 3 runs everywhere, without any plugin or installation, directly in any browser of your choice and on any device you currently use. Webble World also use secure transfer with SSL and https, making everything you do in Webble World as safe and private as basic online communication can be. An additional supportive security feature within the site itself which we call 'Trust' [11] allows users to create a circle of trust in order to safer control which Webbles to use. Sharing is a key element of Webble World, but sometimes one would like to know where specific Webbles come from and who you collaborate with. Higher security and trust-like features have been a request from previous possible industry partners whom have considered using our system for some of their software development.

We believe that with the Webble World approach to software development and user's self-improvement and configuration possibilities we minimize the distance and bridge the gap between traditional users and trained developers to eventually make them one and the same.

2.2 Under the Hood

Webble World 2.5 and earlier versions were dependent on the Silverlight plugin and Microsoft technology to work but the new version has been developed in order to, as far as possible, eliminate any form of 3rd party dependencies and limitations by using the most open, free and standardized technology available.

Server Side. The underlying technology and engine which drives the system of the Webble World server is built with node.js (a JavaScript syntax developing language for server side development). All data managed by the server, like Webbles and users etc. are stored and managed with mongoDB, a very fast non-SQL document database engine.

By choosing node.js and MongoDB the server side is extremely easy to maintain and scale up, as well as to deploy and replicate on any machine with any OS, which is why these particular technologies were chosen, even though others were considered.

For most people this information is completely irrelevant though, since there is no need to set up your own server. All Webble development is done on the client side via the Webble World site deployed by Hokkaido University.

Client Side. Webble World 3 is all HTML5 driven. With 'HTML5' we mean a combination of latest HTML, CSS3 styles and JavaScript.

The main work horse is a JavaScript library called AngularJS, developed by Google which is the nerve system of our creation and the key part to the MVC structure. JavaScript is powerful, though unruly, but with AngularJS, one gets much more structure and control. AngularJS may be seen as 3rd part library of course, but it is deeper embedded and Webble World is not dependent on future changes of the library outside our control, like was the case with MS Silverlight. AngularJS was not the only framework considered initially, but it was by far, the most powerful and innovative as well as user-friendly once the basic foundation of the framework was understood.

As a Webble template developer, one is not demanded to use AngularJS, but it will definitely empower and simplify your coding. One of AngularJS major strengths is the genius separation of the DOM and the application logic. Tutorials on how to master AngularJS may be found online. Webble World also fully supports JQuery for those who are familiar with and fond of that library. Any other JavaScript library or code that exists can be added and used in individual Webbles at the discretion of the developer. No limits.

All configurations and current state of a Webble is stored as JSON data. This is the main file for any Webble because it tells us how a specific Webble is glued together and what parts it needs. The choice to use JSON was primarily made due to its natural connection with JavaScript, node.js and MongoDB. XML was also considered since previous Webble implementations had used it, but was eventually regarded slower in parsing and larger in transfer-size in comparison.

2.3   Core System Description

The features available in Webble World aims to help people design and create their own web experience and tools and easily share it with the rest of the world, all with a minimum of advanced computer skills. Below follows a description of how that is pursued and achieved.

Server Side. There is little one need to know about the server since all its work is automated and all its needed interfaces are moved to the client side, but among its tasks is of course to manage and maintain all Webbles in the system. It also keeps track of individual user's all specific connections to its accounts, groups, Webbles, Workspaces etc., all which is managed via the client or automatically by server-side sensors.

Client Side. When the Webble World 3.0 web site is first loaded the user see a blank work area with a top main menu. In the top right corner, the user can register and/or login, which is a requirement before one can create and save one's own Webbles, but not needed for just loading and using Webbles. User accounts can also be linked to social media accounts for easier access and future interaction and sharing of Webbles to the outside world.

The top menu has five sections; Workspace, Webbles, Edit, View and Help, where Webbles and Edit are the most important. Under 'Webbles' the user can open the Webble Browser where one can search for Webbles for specific purposes, like text Webbles, Image Webbles, Chart Webbles, Window Webbles etc. The search is conducted upon key words, names, descriptions and developer. When a Webble of interest is found the user can load it into the work area via the load button or drag and drop its image (Fig. 2).

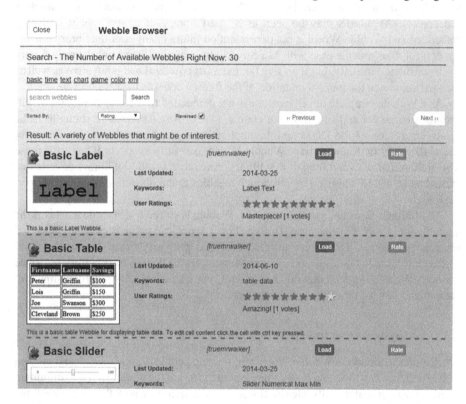

Fig. 2. The Webble Browse and search interface.

Webbles may also be loaded directly as JSON files from the local computer or remote servers, without using the Webble browser, if such files exist.

When one or more Webbles have been loaded, the user can begin to interact with them. There are basically two ways of Webble interaction available.

One is the most obvious, by using the Webble, its intended way as we are taught by previous web software experience, meaning select something in a list, press a button or type text in the text box. This is the common way of interacting with the web with or without Webbles and the result of such interaction depends on the Webble. This approach would be the way to go if one is looking for a specific tool or application and have found such in the Webble browser and now intend to use it as declared.

The other way is to edit, configure and combine the Webble in order to create a new tool or web application, one that maybe does not yet exist in the Webble browser or, one that could be made much better. To do so the Edit part of the main menu will be of use, as well as the Webble's own menu, and if the Execution mode of Webble World 3 is set to 'Developer', which is recommended, also by the use of the Webble attached interaction balls, activated by double click.

The common workflow when creating a new Webble by configuration and combination of existing Webbles is to load the required Webbles into the work surface and then save it as a personal workspace.

A workspace can be saved and loaded via the Workspace section in the menu and will contain those Webbles included by the user. A workspace helps the user to separate Webble projects and applications in personal and private setups and for easy access during development. A workspace can also be easily shared with other Webble users, for collaborative development or real time communication. Changes to a workspace are immediately communicated to all other users in real time. Using a workspace is not required but it simplifies the work, especially when one is working on several Webble projects.

Webble Configuration. As the requested Webbles are loaded the user can begin configure and shape it to his/her current need and also combine them accordingly. For that the 'Edit', Webble pop-up menu or Webble interaction balls are invoked (Fig. 3).

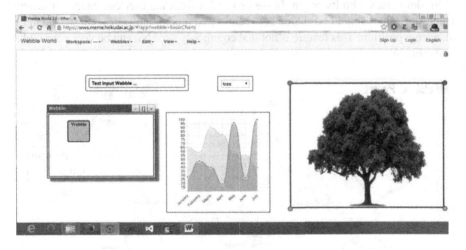

Fig. 3. Webble World 3.0 web interface, with a few different Webbles loaded.

Besides the self-explanatory Webble interactions like 'Delete' and 'Duplicate' the user can edit the Webble properties or slots via the 'Properties' form. There the user can alter any slot value available for wanted effect. Some control the inner logic, while others control the appearance.

If the Webble lacks a slot according to the user, he/she can then add one or more custom slots. There are three types of custom slot available. Either a basic value slot which only has a name and a value (of any type), or a CSS related slot whose value will affect some part of an element of the Webble, or the final one which is called a merged combo slot. A merged combo slot is a slot which carries the values of two or more other slots in one container. This is useful when a Webble needs to communicate several of its values through the chain of relatives. For avoidance of complex connections which is hard to oversee and follow, Webbles can only communicate one slot value to each Webble it is related to. A lot of the time that is sufficient, but in some cases one need to communicate more values, and then the possibility to create a single slot that holds multiple values is very useful.

In order to be able to communicate slot values between Webbles they need to be related in a parent child connection. That is easily done via the Webble menu and a mouse click. When a Webble is connected with another, the user can configure slot communication between them via the child Webble. Via the Webble menu one opens the slot communication form and there select what slot value in the parent and what in the child should communicate and in what direction. If a combo slot is used one can also channel the internal slots of the combo. Many Webbles have a default slot communication that gets enabled as soon as a relationship is created, this is to simplify and speed up default behavior, but the user can change that easily via the Webble menu.

There is another form of relationship and communication available as well which is called 'shared model duplicate'. When that is selected in the Webble menu a duplicate is created of the selected Webble which is not related as a child or parent but still share all its slot values with its origin. In the properties form the user can enable or disable which slot values should be shared between shared model duplicates, but the default is all, except position. This feature is not that commonly used but can be very powerful at times (Fig. 4).

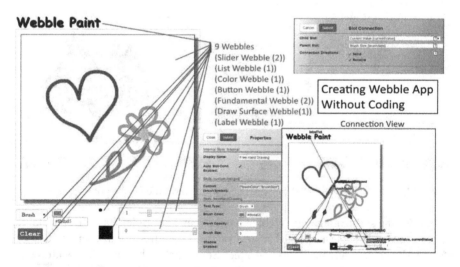

Fig. 4. Load Webbles, configure its slot properties, connect to other Webbles and configure slot communication. Building a paint web app without any code in 15 min.

These fairly simple steps are all it takes; slot value editing, perhaps adding custom slots, parent child connection and slot communication configuration, and perhaps a shared model setup. By using these techniques via simple mouse operations and straight forward keyboard inputs the user can create any complex application or Webble Widget for any type of use (regarding that there are proper Webble templates available).

Webble Deployment. When a Webble is finished, content and behavior wise, the user may want to package and polish the Webble before it is published online. One way to do that is to enable a set of protection flags on the Webble in order to adjust the Webble for its intended use. Such things like locking a Webble from being moved or deleted or showing popup menu can be an important part of getting the Webble to be more user-friendly. The user can also wrap all the contained Webble templates in a bundle in order to hide the internal parts of the Webble. The Bundling process also allows the user to select which slots should be visible and usable from outside to those who load the Webble.

Since Webble world is an open collaborative environment, any protection flag or bundling can always be undone by any other user who wants to experiment or understand the inner workings of a Webble, but for those who do not care for that, they will find a bundled Webble to be much more accessible and user-friendly and easy to use.

The last step is of course to publish the Webble to the online server for others to find in the Webble browser. That process is as simple as all previous ones. Select Publish in the Webble menu, fill in some descriptive data about the Webble to be easy to find and make it look tempting to use and click the submit-button and a second later the world can rejoice in the latest Webble crafting available.

User Management and Support. The user account allows the user to be connected and anonymously identified as the developer of the Webbles he/she have created. It also helps in collaboration between other Webble users as well as in sharing of ones work. The Webble user account can be connected to other social media sites and simplify login and prepare for sharing of posts and Webble updates, though the latter is not fully implemented yet.

An important security feature of Webble world is the concept of groups and trust. Groups are organizations, companies and such which can have additional sub groups which users can join and be a part of and use as a platform which through Webbles are shared and published from. This makes these Webbles not only the responsibility of the developer but also a responsibility of the group. Groups are created and controlled by appointed administrative group managers and not by every user. Users can then select a group and mark it as 'trusted', in order to help the user to select safe and trustworthy Webbles when using Webble World. Trusted Webbles are highlighted in the Webble browser for easy search and Webble World will clearly show and warn the user when a Webble which originates from an untrusted source is present in a Webble compound [11]. Groups also allow member users to share API keys and software licenses used within that group's Webble development.

In the help menu the user will find manuals, support contact info, FAQ and development packages which contains all needed references and information for any form of

Webble development and Webble template creation. There is also a real-time chat available for direct access to other users currently online for fast response and community shared support.

Webble Template Development. In order for Webble World to be really effective and useful for the average Web user there is a need for having many basic Webble building blocks available in the Webble browser, so called Webble templates. These are the smallest parts, the atoms, of Webble World, and they are created with code. One cannot directly see the difference between Webble templates or a compound Webbles in the Webble browser, but the basic concept is that a template Webble is a non-configured and non-combined Webble who cannot be broken apart into smaller parts. It has only been created with ordinary web scripting using JavaScript, CSS and HTML.

Template Webbles are created by web programmers inside the Template Editor section of Webble World, either from scratch or by creating a base foundation from an existing Webble.

Anyone that knows basic JavaScript and HTML can create their own Webble templates, and with the help of the carefully commented default code that is auto generated with each new Webble created and the downloadable reference and development support package, it should be fairly easy for most to learn how to master the process. Users can also benefit from other developers work by creating a template copy based from an already existing Webble, via the 'About' section in the Webble menu. That will minimize the risk of reinventing the wheel as well as making sure Webbles evolve in a more natural way.

In the Template Editor the user can then write the necessary code for the Webbles to be created following the simple guidelines. When a Template is saved it can be loaded into the work surface via the top menu as a 'sandbox-Webble', a Webble which is not yet published and only available to the template developer. A sandbox Webble can still interact with any other Webble the user chose to load for testing and debugging. When the template feels finished and working, the user publish the sandbox Webble the same way he/she would publish any other Webble and make it available to the world in the Webble browser.

In the earlier stages of Webble World 3.0, it will be more common that Webble users will find that the Webble template they need is not yet created, and that is when a new template hopefully will be designed and added, so that future users will less and less often need to include some template development within their Webble project.

Personal Investigation and Webble Application Examples. The best way to fully understand the content of this paper is of course by personal experience and by visiting Webble World 3, and maybe also the older previous version of 2.5, and load interesting Webbles that tickles ones curiosity and use them and maybe even break them apart to see how they were put together.

Since the new version is still very young it does not yet has a large amount of Webbles, especially of the more complex kind, but such can be found and experimented with in the 2.5 version just for reference and understanding. There are all form of widgets, applications, editors, tools and games available; all accessible online by googling Webble World (Fig. 5).

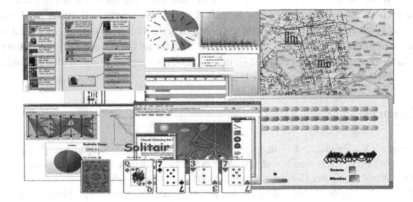

Fig. 5. A multiple range of applications created for Webble World 2.5, soon also in 3.0

When one is ready to start developing one's own Webbles, one will quickly notice that the time needed to create a Webble application in comparison to a traditional Web- or desktop application is highly reduced, and the more stand-alone parts that becomes available the quicker the development will be.

3   Summary

Webble World 3.0 is a web top development and visualization tool based on meme media architecture that view all web content and its peripheral infrastructure as standalone objects which can be manipulated, rearranged and personalized as easy as one would edit a text document with basic mouse operations and simple keyboard inputs. It is available online, open and free for anyone who wants to try, individuals or organizations, at the following web address: https://wws.meme.hokudai.ac.jp/.

Webble World 3.0 aims to make software application development a more globally shared effort that involves people also outside the realm of programmers and to minimize the time and workload of making software due to the capabilities to adapt, adjust, modify and combine freely already fully working and available building blocks.

Webble World 3 is reaching to bridge the distance between those who use the web and those who develop it and make them work closer together in a worldwide collaboration between both friends and strangers, and maybe even making them become one and the same.

The current version of Webble World is designed based on a combination of original theoretical concepts of IntelligentPad and Meme Media architecture, modern web technology practices, frameworks and libraries together with unofficial user queries. No official user survey has yet been done for any version of Webble World.

Software users have often been very frustrated of the fact that they are in the hands of developers who do not fully understand the need of the user, and developers are often forced to develop systems they do not care for, just because they have programming skills. With Webble World 3.0 we believe that much of that frustration can be cured. Those who have the skill for coding can write the building blocks and templates that tickle their interest, focusing on the technical details and narrowed down problem of their fancy, while the classic software users can then on their own put together their own personal applications, tweaked and configure exactly as they want without having to learn how to write computer code or sit in long development meetings trying to communicate a vision they already see so clearly.

References

1. Tanaka, Y., Imataki, T.: IntelligentPad: a hypermedia system allowing functional composition of active media objects through direct manipulations. In: Proceedings of the IFIP 11th World Computer Congress, San Francisco, pp. 541–546 (1989)
2. Tanaka, Y.: Meme Media and Meme Market Architectures: Knowledge Media for Editing, Distributing and Managing Intellectual Resources. IEEE Press & Wiley-Interscience, Los Alamitos (2003)
3. Dawkins, R.: The Selfish Gene. Oxford University Press, Oxford (1976)
4. Blackmore, S.: The Meme Machine. Oxford University Press, Oxford (1999)
5. Fujima, J.: A Unified Framework for Organizing, Accessing, and Federating Web Resources. Hokkaido University, Sapporo (2006)
6. Tanaka, Y.: Knowledge federation over the web based on meme media technologies. In: Jantke, K.P., Lunzer, A., Spyratos, N., Tanaka, Y. (eds.) Federation over the Web. LNCS (LNAI), vol. 3847, pp. 159–182. Springer, Heidelberg (2006)
7. Tanaka, Y.: Meme media and a world-wide meme pool. In: Proceedings of the Fourth ACM International Conference on Multimedia, pp. 175–186. ACM (1996)
8. Kuwahara, M., Tanaka, Y.: Advanced "Webble" application development directly in the browser by utilizing the full power of meme media customization and event management capabilities. In: ICME 2012, IEEE International Conference on MULTIMEDIA AND EXPO, TEMPEKU Workshop: Tangible Edutainment Media for Playful Evolution of Knowledge and Understanding, Melbourne, pp. 211–216, July 2012
9. Kuwahara, M.: The power of Webble world and how to utilize it. In: Arnold, O., Spickermann, W., Spyratos, N., Tanaka, Y. (eds.) WWS 2013. CCIS, vol. 372, pp. 31–55. Springer, Heidelberg (2013)
10. Kuwahara, M., Tanaka, Y.: The mindset of a Webble world citizen: developing applications in a meme media environment. In: Arnold, O., Spickermann, W., Spyratos, N., Tanaka, Y. (eds.) WWS 2013. CCIS, vol. 372, pp. 56–65. Springer, Heidelberg (2013)
11. Georgalis, Y., Tanaka, Y.: Towards trusting user-generated content in web applications. In: ASE BigData/SocialInformatics/PASSAT/BioMedCom Conference 2014, Harvard University, 14–16 December 2014. ISBN:978-1-62561-003-4

Cloud Based Processing Services Based on Linked Data

Elias Grinias[3][(✉)] and Dimitris Kotzinos[1,2]

[1] ETIS Laboratory ENSEA UCP CNRS UMR 8501,
Department of Computer Science,
University of Cergy-Pontoise, Cergy-Pontoise, France
Dimitrios.Kotzinos@u-cergy.fr
[2] Institute of Computer Science,
Foundation for Research and Technology–Hellas (FORTH-ICS), Hellas, Greece
[3] Department of Civil Engineering, Surveying Engineering and Geoinformatics,
Technological Educational Institute of Central Macedonia, Serres, Greece
grinias@teiser.gr

Abstract. Cloud computing is providing a computing infrastructure to facilitate storage and processing of massive amounts of information (Big Data). Processing of massive datasets becomes more and more important since the data becoming available to us increase every day in volume, variety, speed of change and (potentially) quality. Processing these data becomes more and more difficult under traditional computing platforms since we need the ability to compute and scale at the same time. Under this context, for this work we describe the design and implementation of a responsive and user driven processing service. This is a geoprocessing service that operates on geospatial datasets and provides geostatistical interpolation (a specific variant called Kriging). This service is based on existing service implementation standards in the geospatial domain (namely WPS standard from OGC). Additionally our service can query and retrieve information that is integrated following the Linked Open Data (LOD) initiative. This is a unique capability that allows the service to rely on data, besides the existing ones and the ones provided by the user, that can be retrieved from the integrated information space that is being built on the web. In this paper we present the design and implementation of the service on a Linked Data store and discuss capabilities, issues and future research.

1 Introduction

Geoprocessing is considered a rather complex and computationally demanding processing activity regardless of the exact type of computation it involves; mainly we refer to statistical geoprocessing including various types of interpolation, that are of interest in this work. Given also the fact that geoprocessing refers to processing of geodatasets, which are usually of high volume, one can assume that this kind of processing is complex due to both computational complexity and data volume reasons.

© Springer International Publishing Switzerland 2016
D. Kotzinos et al. (Eds.): ISIP 2014, CCIS 497, pp. 97–112, 2016.
DOI: 10.1007/978-3-319-38901-1_7

On the other hand cloud computing promises scalable and elastic resources both for processing and storage of data. This has made many researchers to consider the cloud as one perfect match for solve complex geoprocessing problems that also need to be applied on large geospatial datasets. Many interesting works in this area exist already. One could reference the work of [17,18] and by [12] where a discussion takes place on how cloud computing can be used and shaped by the spatial sciences. Works like [16,19] shape the ground for a more in depth look into the algorithmic or technical needs of the geospatial cloud based applications. A very interesting comparison of various cloud based geospatial solutions can be found at [17]; although the authors are focused on Windows Azure and Google Application Engine platforms, the works compared are rather comprehensive and the conclusions can be extended to other cloud platforms like Amazon Web Services (AWS)[1], which is the one used for the work presented in this paper. In this respect our proposal is similar and complementary of those efforts, since (as we detail in Sects. 2, 3 and 4) we provide a standards based geoprocessing implementation and infrastructure.

At the same time an effort is underway to create more interconnected data sets; it has been evident that data published on the web cannot be fully exploited if they remain stored in information silos where no one but the owner will have access to. This effort claims better results if our data are created, published and re-used as Linked Data (LD), i.e., data that are inter-linked with each other and can be uniquely identified based on unique URIs. LD and the technology supporting them not only enables their re-use and interconnection but also allows for combining them on the fly, which adds value to the data and highlights and promotes their potential. In fact, nowadays, a great amount of LD is actually freely available and open on the web, thus leading to the Linked Open Data (LOD) concept. Such data are available for various areas either in raw RDF form or via SPARQL endpoints. The work presented on this paper provides geoprocessing facilities for Linked Open Data stored in an RDF triplestore in the cloud. Thus to the best of our knowledge is the only work, which actually retrieves and processes Linked Open GeoData by keeping both the data and the processing in the cloud.

The paper is organized as follows: Sect. 2 describes the preliminaries for the understanding of the Web Processing Service standards; Sect. 3 discusses the theoretical part of the specific geoprocessing algorithm used for statistical interpolation of values, called Kriging; Sect. 4 describes the implementation of Kriging/geoprocessing services according to the standards while Sect. 5 details the Linked Open Data (LOD) infrastructure and capabilities. In Sect. 6 the client that has been implemented to provide geoprocessing capabilities on Linked Open geodata is presented. The paper concludes with some conclusions and pointers for future work in Sect. 7.

---

[1] http://aws.amazon.com/.

2   Open Geospatial Consortium Web Processing Service

Web services are defined as software systems that allow the interaction between machines over a network. In such systems, there is often a machine-readable description of the operations offered by the service and the other systems communicate with the service using messages formatted in markup languages such as XML.

Web Processing Service (WPS) [7] is an Open Geospatial Consortium (OGC)[2] standard, which provides rules for standardizing the implementation of geographic calculations ("processes") as a web service. More specifically, the standard

- describes inputs and outputs (requests and responses) for invoking geospatial processing services, as a Web service,
- defines the way that a client can request the execution of a process, and how the output from the process is handled and
- defines an interface that facilitates the publishing of geospatial processes and clients discovery of and binding to those processes.

The Web Processing Service (WPS) standard defines three operations:

- **GetCapabilities** that returns metadata describing the service capabilities,
- **DescribeProcess** that returns a description of a process including its inputs and outputs and
- **Execute**, which returns the output(s) of a process.

In practice, WPS operations are invoked by submitting XML to the URL of the service. When requesting an Execute operation the HTTP request identifies the inputs, the name of process to be executed, and the form of output to be provided after execution. Data are often embedded in process execution input/output XML, although references to web-accessible data inputs/outputs are supported as well.

Input/output data required by the WPS can be delivered across the network or they can be available at the server. Three types of data are defined by the standard, namely:

- **Complex Data** such as imagery, XML, CSV, and custom (or proprietary) data structures,
- **Literal Data** for numerical values or strings and
- **Bounding Box** Data type for the geographic coordinates of a rectangular area.

3   Geoprocessing

3.1   Preliminaries

Kriging is a geostatistical method, which relies on the fact that as distance between points increases, the similarity, defined by the covariance or correlation

---

[2] http://www.opengeospatial.org/.

between points, decreases. Kriging predicts the unknown value $Z(\mathbf{x}_0)$ at a location in question $\mathbf{x}_0$ based on the data values in a neighborhood of this location. Similarly to other well known interpolation techniques, the calculation of the unknown value is based on a weighted sum of the locations with known values in the neighborhood of point $\mathbf{x}_0$:

$$\hat{Z}(\mathbf{x}_0) = \sum_{i=1}^{n} w_i(\mathbf{x}_0) Z(\mathbf{x}_i) \tag{1}$$

where weight $w_i(\mathbf{x}_0)$ is the contribution of value $Z(\mathbf{x}_i)$ and $n = N(\mathbf{x}_0)$ is the number of neighbors involved in predicting the unknown value. Unlike the deterministic interpolation methods, in Kriging the input data values are considered to be the realization $z(\mathbf{x})$ of a random field $Z(\mathbf{x})$ which consists of a trend $m(\mathbf{x})$ and a residual $R(\mathbf{x})$:

$$Z(\mathbf{x}) = m(\mathbf{x}) + R(\mathbf{x})$$

or

$$R(\mathbf{x}) = Z(\mathbf{x}) - m(\mathbf{x})$$

Kriging estimates the residual $R(\mathbf{x})$ as the weighted sum of the residuals at adjacent positions around the location point $\mathbf{x}$. Weights $w_i(\cdot)$ of Eq. (1) are derived from the covariance or the semivariance of known values and therefore semivariance modeling should statistically characterize the residual component.

The three basic variations of Kriging, namely Simple, Ordinary and Universal (or with trend), arise from the assumptions made about the trend component of input data as being known and constant (Simple), unknown and locally constant (Ordinary) and spatially or functionally varying (Universal Kriging), respectively. Both Simple and Ordinary techniques may be considered sub-cases of Universal Kriging. In addition, if the trend of Universal Kriging is not a function of spatial coordinates, then other known Kriging interpolation variants arise, such as Kriging with External Drift. Finally, if prediction refers to the average of the measured values in a particular area rather than to single points, we have the so-called Block Kriging.

3.2   Ordinary Kriging Method Analysis

Kriging interpolation consists of two steps, namely:

1. covariance, or semivariance modeling based on the set of locations with known values and
2. prediction of values for a number of points in question.

Semivariance Modeling. Kriging uses semivariance to express the degree of relationship between points on a surface. The empirical semivariance is half the variance of the differences between all possible points spaced a constant distance (lag) h apart:

$$\hat{\gamma}(h) = \frac{1}{2n(h)} \sum_{i=1}^{n(h)} (z(\mathbf{x}_i) - z(\mathbf{x}_i + \mathbf{h}))^2 \tag{2}$$

Semivariogram plots (empirical) semivariance values against lags h of distance. In practice, instead of the often noisy semivariance measurements which are obtained using Eq. (2) on the points with known values, a semivariance model, or function of the three parameters, *Range*, *Sill* and *Nugget* defined below, is used to compute the semivariance of point pairs according to their distance.

In theory, the semivariance value at the origin ($h = 0$) should be zero. If it is significantly different from zero for distances very close to zero, then this minimum semivariance value is referred to as the *Nugget* (Fig. 1). As points are compared to increasingly distant points, the semivariance increases. Beyond some distance, called *Range*, the values of any points on the surface are statistically uncorrelated. The semivariance value at $h = Range$ is called *Sill*.

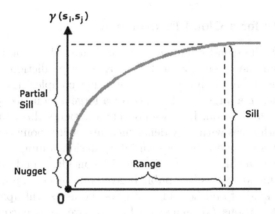

Fig. 1. Semivariogram and *Range*, *Nugget*, *Sill* (from ArcGIS Help 10.1: Semivariogram and covariance functions).

Prediction. Prediction may involve the overall set, or a subset of points with known values. In the first case we have global prediction. In the second case, a subset of points with known values is defined in an area of an acceptable, user-given radius (*SearchRadius*) around the point in question and only this subject is used for prediction (local neighborhood prediction). Furthermore, if the cardinality of this subset is less than a user-given value *MinNum*, no prediction is made ("bulls eyes" effect) and if exceeds a user-given value *MaxNum*, then only the *MaxNum* points, which are closest to the point in question will be used in prediction. Furthermore, *MaxNum* can be used on its own, without using search radius at all.

The steps taken to predict the unknown value at a specific location $\mathbf{x}_0$, given the set of points with known values are as follows:

1. First, distances between point $\mathbf{x}_0$ and each point with known value are computed.

2. Based on those distances, semivariance values between x_0 and each one of the points with known values are computed, using the semivariance model.
3. Given the semivariance values, a series of linear equations is solved in order to get the predicted value for the location in question.

In case of using local neighborhood prediction, the steps above involve only the points that are placed in the local neighborhood of x_0.

Furthermore, in most cases, interpolation refers to the prediction of values in locations of a grid that includes the points with known values. The parameters for grid construction, namely, grid extent in each dimension and grid cell size, may be given by the user or (grid extent for example), could be extracted automatically from the locations of points with known values.

3.3   Suitability for a Cloud Environment

As noted earlier, the cloud offers scalable unlimited (but not free) processing capabilities. From the discussion so far on Kriging prediction, one can notice that although the solving of linear equations is not complex, the execution time easily increases when a large set of points (or a large area in geospatial terms) is involved in the computation. In nowadays environments this can easily happen since we have both areas with very dense measurements (points) and large areas (e.g. Europe) where we need to perform interpolation computations.

As seen though in this work, we should also consider an additional factor for the increased demand: if this is a publicly available service we have literally no control on what kind of and how big datasets the users will upload in order to perform their calculations. Given also the fact that we might encounter situations where many concurrent users might want to use the service at the same time we could phase situations where a significant number of computations will take place at the same time but also on demand. These situations match perfectly the computational model of the cloud and thus make these services suitable for cloud based implementation.

4   Design and Implementation of a Geoprocessing Cloud Based Service

4.1   Open Source Kriging Implementations

In what follows, we refer to open source libraries or executable programs that provide Kriging interpolation implementations.

SAGA and SEXTANTE. The geospatial analysis library SAGA (System for Automated Geoscientific Analyses) [2] is implemented in C++ and includes processing modules for modeling the variograms as well as for performing Ordinary and Universal Kriging. The SEXTANTE (Sistema EXtremeño de ANálisis TErritorial) [13] library (coded in Java) includes the same functionality with SAGA, considering Kriging interpolation.

geoR. geoR [11] is a package of the open source, statistical processing environment R [10]. geoR includes modules for variogram modeling, as well as for applying Simple, Ordinary, Universal and external drift Kriging interpolation. The package is used by the v.Krige function of GRASS GIS [4], for applying Kriging techniques on input vector data.

HGPL. The HPGL (High Performance Geostatistics Library) library [5] (implemented in Python and C++) includes functions for variogram modeling and for applying simple, ordinary and generalized Kriging interpolation in the form of locally variable means. Data input as well as output results are stored in grids, as Eclipse Property or GSLIB [3] text files. Furthermore, the algorithms are applied on the Cartesian grid (IJK-grid) and the linear equations of Kriging techniques are solved using LAPACK solvers [1].

Gstat. Gstat [8] is a program dedicated to multivariable geostatistical modeling, prediction and simulation. It consists of a broad range of functionalities, which permit the efficient development of Kriging interpolation techniques. It was originally (1997) developed in ANSI C but, since 2003, its functionalities are available as an R package as well [9].

4.2   Servers and OGC-WPS Implementation

Among the many open source implementations of Kriging prediction available on the web, we selected the R [10] implementation of the Gstat [8] library (R-Gstat)[9] for performing Ordinary Kriging. Considering interpolation, R-Gstat supports

- Simple, Ordinary, Generalized as well as Block based Kriging prediction,
- global or local-neighborhood prediction,
- prediction on non-projected data using great circle distance between known points and
- fast enough prediction, since its main functionality is coded in C and local-neighborhood prediction is based on a fast neighborhood search algorithm.

WPS Ordinary Kriging process has been implemented using only open source software written in Java. The basic components of the overall system at server side (Fig. 2) are the Web Java Server and a WPS Java Container (implementation) installed in server's workspace, which provides the necessary functionality to handle responses to clients' requests for WPS processes' description/execution, according to the OGC-WPS standard. This way, developers are free to implement and publish web processes without having to worry about client/server interface and WPS processes' input/output issues.

Kriging process has been implemented as a Java class in a Linux machine, using Apache Tomcat[3] Web Java Server and the 52 North WPS[4] 3.1.1 implementation of OGC-WPS 1.0.0 standard [7]. Ordinary Kriging is applied on input data

---

[3] http://tomcat.apache.org/.
[4] http://52north.org/communities/geoprocessing/wps.

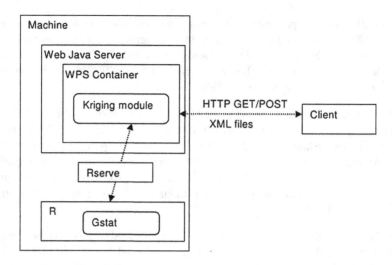

Fig. 2. Server configuration of WPS Kriging Implementation.

using R Gstat package. The interconnection between the Java module located at the WPS Container and R is handled by the TCP/IP server Rserve [15]. Rserve forwards to R the Java-R Interface (JRI) [14] instructions of the Java Kriging module and sends back to the module the returned output of each R instruction (if such an output exists), as it is depicted in the inner frame **Kriging Execution** of Fig. 5.

4.3   Geospatial Interpolation Process Implementation

The input of the process is handled by the WPS Container and consists of:

1. The input vector data (or layer) in the form of

$$[x, y, feature_1, feature_2, ..., feature_M]$$

   tuples, where $\mathbf{x} = (x, y)$ are the locations of vectors.
2. The field ($feature_j$) upon which Ordinary Kriging will be applied. It has to be a feature with arithmetic (real or integer) values.
3. The semivariance model that will be used. Corresponds to one of the variogram models supported by R Gstat.
4. The *Nugget*, *Sill* and *Range* values.
5. The *SearchRadius* value, measured in kilometers for non-projected input data and in meters otherwise.
6. The *MinNum* and *MaxNum* values.
7. The cell size that will be used for constructing the grid with predicted values. Cell size should be given in meters for projected data and in degrees otherwise.

The Coordinate Reference System (CRS) of input vector data is assumed to be included in input data and if not, CRS EPSG:4326 (WGS84) is used by default. Grid extent is automatically computed by the extent of the corresponding input data.

The results of Kriging are three files, accessible as temporary links. The first file includes the kriging predictions in tab separated values (tsv) format, the second one is an image preview of Kriging predictions in PNG format and the third is a tsv file of the input data in $[x, y, feature_j]$ format. The first file includes Kriging predictions in the form $[x, y, predicted\_value, prediction\_variance]$ which (as it is depicted in the inner frame **Kriging Execution** of Fig. 5) after Gstat execution

1. are returned as R object in the opposite direction from R to the Java module through Rserve,
2. they are converted to Java arrays and
3. are written in the tsv file.

The second file is created by a plot function of R and is returned to the Java Server as well, using the file transfer capabilities of Rserve. The third file is constructed by the WPS at the Java Server side using the input data of the process. The OGC-WPS output XML (i.e. the response of **Execute** operation), which includes the three temporary links is then asynchronously returned to the client by the WPS Container.

5   Linked Open Geodata on the Cloud

There have been only limited efforts to publish Linked Open Geodata on the cloud. [6] provide a comparison among different efforts of publishing linked geodata on the cloud platforms and provide the description of an elastic and scalable service based infrastructure for providing Data-As-A-Service capabilities to any platform wishing to extend its application in Linked Data environments. The Linked Data Management API proposed in [6] carries very promising capabilities and allows for a seamless integration of the available Linked Data in various applications; its main architecture is depicted in Fig. 3.

One of the applications built on top of the LOD Management System is the Geoprocessing service, which has been described above, that retrieves data from the RDF Triplestore through the Linked Data API. Data are returned in RDF/XML format and then processed through the appropriate methods of the Geoprocessing Web Service. Querying the RDF Triplestore has been seamless and we had no actual trouble in retrieving the information in this format. Linked Data offer the opportunity to the geoprocessing module to combine data coming from different sources but refer to the specific area of interest. In that respect data coming from diverse sources can be easily integrated without the need of expensive (and most of the times incomplete) integration. The geoprocessing service will also use the Linked Data triplestore to store users own data that (s)he needs to upload in order to provide more input for better calculations. These data if described correctly using the appropriate ontology (-ies) can then

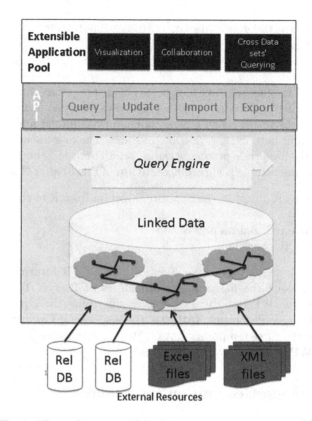

Fig. 3. The architecture of the LOD management system [6].

be linked with other data about the same area, allowing the scientists to draw better and more educated conclusions.

Up to its current implementation the service exploits the cloud only by allowing spawning of more instances in cases the load of the geoprocessing server becomes too big. Thus we use the standard AWS load balancer to account for high traffic or exceeding computational requirements (especially in cases of very complex statistical computations).

6   Client Application

For testing the WPS process and demonstrating its usage, a web client[5] has been implemented by modifying the open source 52 North Openlayers WPS Client[6]. In Fig. 5, the sequence diagram of client-server interaction is depicted in order to perform Kriging on Linked Open geodata using the web process implemented. In accordance with that Figure, the sequence of actions is as follows:

---

[5] http://portal.ingeoclouds.eu/sitools/client-user/Geoprocessing/project-index.html.
[6] https://wiki.52north.org/bin/view/Processing/52nOpenLayersWPSClient.

User Access. When the user navigates to the URL of client, (s)he sees the central html page built using styles and JavaScript (JS) libraries.

WPS Description. A panel has been developed as Openlayers control for giving the ability to the user to select input layer and Kriging parameters. To construct the panel, an HTTP GET request is send to the WPS container issuing the description of Kriging web process in terms of data inputs and parameters required for its execution (**DescribeProcess** operation). The response to that request is the OGC-WPS XML description file, which, after its asynchronous arrival at the client, is parsed in order to construct the panel (Fig. 4). WPS description step is executed upon loading of the main html page, and may be ignored in the case of a WPS with only one process. However, having available a mechanism of dynamically constructing the panel based on the DescribeProcess operation of OGC-WPS standard, leads to a highly extendable WPS client (e.g. in case of changing parameters of an already implemented process or of publishing new WPS processes).

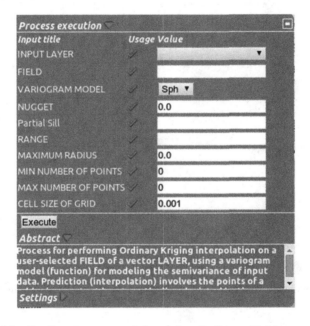

Fig. 4. User friendly Openlayers panel for giving Ordinary Kriging prediction input parameters.

Vector Layer Loading on Map. In current implementation, the user selects predefined queries, which are treated as "vector layers" of the Openlayers[7] library. Each time the user selects to load on the map a layer of that kind (using

---

[7] http://openlayers.org/.

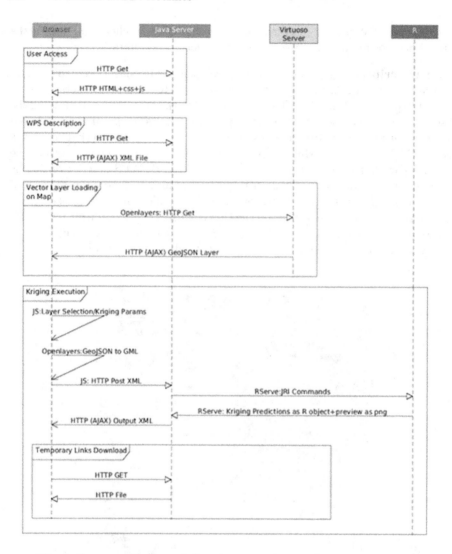

Fig. 5. Sequence diagram of client/server and server/R interconnections.

the JS control unit depicted in Fig. 6), a SPARQL[8] query is sent to Virtuoso[9] Server as HTTP POST request. The response is the result-set of the query which

1. is (asynchronously) sent back to Openlayers in GeoJSON[10] format,
2. is then transformed to an Openlayers layer and this layer is displayed on the Openlayers map and

---

[8] http://www.w3.org/TR/rdf-sparql-query/.
[9] http://virtuoso.openlinksw.com/.
[10] http://geojson.org/.

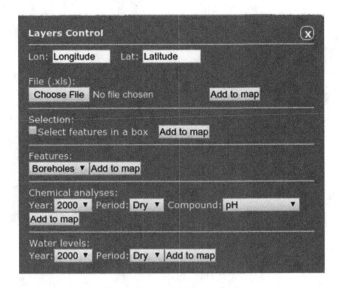

Fig. 6. Panel for loading vector layers on map. The user is given the ability to load (1) his own data in excel format, (3) linked geodata fetched from Virtuoso server using fixed SPARQL queries and (4),(5) linked geodata fetched from Virtuoso server using partially parameterized SPARQL queries. In addition, the user can create new vector layers using the rectangle box tool (2).

3. the corresponding entry of WPS panel with the layers that may be used as input data for Kriging is properly updated with the layer just loaded on the map.

Other sources of data could be used as well. Current implementation supports the loading on map of user data stored in Excel format. The procedure followed in that case is exactly the same: Excel data are first transformed to GeoJSON format and are then rendered on map as Openlayers vector layers. Furthermore, a tool has been implemented that permits the selection of features in a rectangle box. Using this tool the user can create new (Openlayers vector) layers from already loaded (on map) ones.

Kriging Execution. First, the user selects one of the loaded layers as the input data layer of the process and gives Kriging specific parameters. Then, the Openlayers layer is transformed to a format acceptable by 52 North OGC-WPS Java implementation (GML 2.0 in current implementation). The OGC-WPS input XML is then constructed, using the input data and Kriging parameters and is forwarded to the process through an HTTP POST request (**Execute** operation). The output XML is parsed using JavaScript and, after all, the user is given the ability by the user-interface to download the output files as described in the **Temporary Links Download** inner frame of the sequence diagram. In Fig. 7(b), the preview PNG image is shown, as it is returned by the WPS

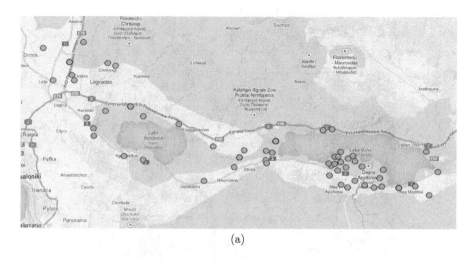

(a)

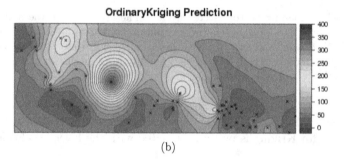

(b)

Fig. 7. (a) Selected input layer (yellow points) and (b) preview of final interpolation result returned by the WPS process. Black crosses in (b) correspond to input data points. (Color figure online)

Ordinary Kriging interpolation process, applied on the selected input layer of Fig. 7(a).

7 Conclusions and Future Work

In this paper we introduced a Cloud based Processing Service that uses a Linked Open Data repository to retrieve its data and store user provided datasets. The service operates on a cloud environment and exploits the elasticity and scalability of the cloud mainly in the form of provision of more instances for processing when needed (scalability) and of storing the users datasets. The service uses Linked Open Data on the cloud, which is a unique feature of this work.

In the future we would like to explore techniques like Map Reduce that allow for distributed geoprocessing, something that in the case of Kriging for example would considerably improve its performance. Additionally we would like to expand the service in order to provide geoprocessing on data that are automatically retrieved through their links on the web. Finally we would like to add more geoprocessing algorithms running in a cloud environment and run benchmarks to determine the differences in performance, scalability, elasticity and reliability between existing solutions and the cloud based one.

Acknowledgements. This work was partially supported by the INGEOCLOUDS project (Project reference: 297300) under the CIP-ICT-PSP.2011.4.1.

References

1. Anderson, E., Bai, Z., Bischof, C., Blackford, L.S., Demmel, J., Dongarra, J.J., Du Croz, J., Hammarling, S., Greenbaum, A., McKenney, A., Sorensen, D.: LAPACK Users' Guide. Society for Industrial and Applied Mathematics, 3rd edn. SIAM, Philadelphia (1999)
2. Böhner, J., McCloy, K.R., Strobl, J. (eds.): SAGA - Analysis and Modelling Applications, vol. 115. Verlag Erich Goltze GmbH, Göttingen (2006)
3. Deutsch, C.V., Journel, A.G.: GSLIB : Geostatistical Software Library and User's Guide. Oxford University Press, New York, Oxford (1992). http://opac.inria.fr/record=b1101614
4. GRASS Development Team: Geographic Resources Analysis Support System (GRASS GIS) Software. Open Source Geospatial Foundation (2012). http://grass.osgeo.org
5. HPGL Development Team: High Performance Geostatistics Library (HPGL) User Guide (2010). http://sourceforge.net/projects/hpgl
6. Kritikos, K., Rousakis, Y., Kotzinos, D.: Linked open geodata management in the cloud. In: Proceedings of the 2nd International Workshop on Open Data, WOD 2013, pp. 3: 1–3: 6 (2013)
7. OGC: OpenGIS Web Processing Service 1.0.0 (2007), openGISStandard, OGC05–007r7. http://www.opengeospatial.org/standards/wps
8. Pebesma, E., Wesseling, C.G.: Gstat: a program for geostatistical modelling, prediction and simulation. Comput. Geosci. **24**(1), 17–31 (1998). http://dx.org/10.1016/s0098-3004(97)00082-4
9. Pebesma, E.J.: Multivariable geostatistics in S: the gstat package. Comput. Geosci. **30**, 683–691 (2004)
10. Development Core Team, R.: R: A Language and Environment for Statistical Computing. R Foundation for Statistical Computing, Vienna, Austria (2011). ISBN3-900051-07-0. http://www.R-project.org/
11. Ribeiro Jr., P., Diggle, P.: geoR: a package for geostatistical analysis. R-NEWS **1**(2), 15–18 (2001). http://cran.R-project.org/doc/Rnews
12. Schäffer, B., Baranski, B., Foerster, T.: Towards spatial data infrastructures in the clouds. In: Painho, M., Santos, M.Y., Pundt, H. (eds.) Geospatial Thinking. LNGC, pp. 399–418. Springer, Berlin, Heidelberg (2010)
13. SEXTANTE development team: Sextante project official website (2011). http://www.sextantegis.com
14. Urbanek, S.: rJava: Low-level R to Java interface (2011). http://CRAN.R-project.org/package=rJava, r package version 0.9-3

15. Urbanek, S.: Rserve: Binary R server (2011). http://CRAN.R-project.org/package=Rserve, r package version 0.6-6
16. Wang, Y., Wang, S., Zhou, D.: Retrieving and indexing spatial data in the cloud computing environment. In: Jaatun, M.G., Zhao, G., Rong, C. (eds.) Cloud Computing. LNCS, vol. 5931, pp. 322–331. Springer, Heidelberg (2009)
17. Yang, C., Goodchild, M., Huang, Q., Nebert, D., Raskin, R., Xu, Y., Bambacus, M., Fay, D.: Spatial cloud computing: How can geospatial sciences use and help shape cloud computing. Int. J. Digit. Earth 4(4), 305–329 (2011)
18. Yang, C., Raskin, R., Goodchild, M., Gahegan, M.: Geospatial cyberinfrastructure: Past, present and future. Comput. Environ. Urban Syst. 34(4), 264–277 (2010)
19. Yue, P., Gong, J., Di, L., Yuan, J., Sun, L., Sun, Z., Wang, Q.: Geopw: Laying blocks for the geospatial processing web. Trans. GIS 14(6), 755–772 (2010)

Author Index

Alkhouli, Abdulhafiz 35

Borzic, Boris 35

Ghariani, Abir 66
Grinias, Elias 97

Hilali, Ines 51

Jen, Tao-Yuan 51, 66

Kotzinos, Dimitris 97
Kuwahara, Micke 85

Laurent, Dominique 51

Marinica, Claudia 51, 66

Nourine, Lhouari 23

Petit, Jean Marc 23

Sacharidis, Dimitris 3
Sellis, Timos 3

Tanaka, Yuzuru 85

Vodislav, Dan 35

Yahia, Sadok Ben 51

Printed in the United States
By Bookmasters